MOVING BEYOND BUSY

Focusing School Change on **Why, What, and How**

GREG CURTIS
FOREWORD BY JAY McTIGHE

Solution Tree | Press

Copyright © 2020 by Solution Tree Press

Materials appearing here are copyrighted. With one exception, all rights are reserved. Readers may reproduce only those pages marked "Reproducible." Otherwise, no part of this book may be reproduced or transmitted in any form or by any means (electronic, photocopying, recording, or otherwise) without prior written permission of the publisher.

555 North Morton Street
Bloomington, IN 47404
800.733.6786 (toll free) / 812.336.7700
FAX: 812.336.7790

email: info@SolutionTree.com
SolutionTree.com

Visit **go.SolutionTree.com/leadership** to download the free reproducibles in this book.

Printed in the United States of America

Library of Congress Cataloging-in-Publication Data

Names: Curtis, Greg, 1950- author.
Title: Moving beyond busy : focusing school change on why, what, and how /
   Greg Curtis.
Description: Bloomington, IN : Solution Tree Press, [2020] | Includes
   bibliographical references and index.
Identifiers: LCCN 2019006825 | ISBN 9781947604575 (perfect bound)
Subjects: LCSH: School improvement programs--United States. | Educational
   change--United States. | Education--Aims and objectives--United States.
Classification: LCC LB2822.82 .C87 2020 | DDC 371.2/07--dc23
LC record available at https://lccn.loc.gov/2019006825

Solution Tree
Jeffrey C. Jones, CEO
Edmund M. Ackerman, President

Solution Tree Press
President and Publisher: Douglas M. Rife
Associate Publisher: Sarah Payne-Mills
Art Director: Rian Anderson
Managing Production Editor: Kendra Slayton
Production Editor: Laurel Hecker
Content Development Specialist: Amy Rubenstein
Copy Editor: Jessi Finn
Proofreader: Elisabeth Abrams
Text and Cover Designer: Abigail Bowen
Editorial Assistant: Sarah Ludwig

For my parents, Joan and Bruce Curtis, who supported me as I tried to figure out who I was and what I might do in this world. The road wasn't straight, but your support helped me explore the possibilities . . . I thank you for that.

ACKNOWLEDGMENTS

I would like to acknowledge the early readers of this book: Dave Beckstead, Matt Merritt, and Patrice Ball. Your guidance in how to tame this beast is greatly appreciated.

I cannot overstate the importance of the support and encouragement of my friend and mentor, Jay McTighe. Your kindness, intellect, and humanity add great depth to your stature in the field and to me personally.

For my wife, Cindy, and my two sons, Max and Ethan—I thank you for putting up with my fretting over this book for so long.

Finally, I'd like to thank Amy Rubenstein, Kendra Slayton, and the good people at Solution Tree for their extraordinary assistance in the development and refinement of this book. You are a pleasure to work with.

Solution Tree Press would like to thank the following reviewers:

Mandy Barrett
Principal
Gravette Upper Elementary School
Gravette, Arkansas

David Pillar
Principal
Jackson Creek Middle School
Bloomington, Indiana

David Huber
Principal
South Side School
Bristol, Connecticut

Julie Wallace
Principal
Quitman Elementary School
Quitman, Arkansas

Andrew Mather
Principal
Karen Western Elementary School
Omaha, Nebraska

Visit **go.SolutionTree.com/leadership** to download
the free reproducibles in this book.

TABLE OF CONTENTS

Reproducibles are in italics.

About the Author xi

Foreword xiii

Introduction 1
    A Framework for Effective Transformation 2
    The *Why*, *What*, and *How* of Change 3
    The Structure of This Book 5
    The Goal of This Book 6

Chapter 1
Why: Identifying Problems With the Traditional Approach to Change 9
    The Problem With Change Implementation 11
    The Problem With Missions and Visions 12
    The Problem With Strategic Plans 14
    Conclusion 17
    Chapter 1 Resources 18

Chapter 2
What: Realigning Thought and Action 21
    Defining Input-Output-Impact 21
        Impacts 22
        Outputs 24
        Inputs 24
    Supporting Planning With I-O-I 24

Driving Action With I-O-I.................................26
    School District of Greenfield........................29
    EdLeader21.....................................30
    Beijing City International School.....................31
    New England Association of Schools and Colleges'
    Commission on International Education................33
Conclusion..34
Chapter 2 Resources...................................35

Chapter 3
How: Putting Impacts at the Center 39
Focus on the Future...................................40
Clarify Goals..43
Operationalize Impacts.................................45
    Performance Areas................................47
    Performance Indicators.............................48
Conclusion..50
Chapter 3 Resources...................................51

Chapter 4
How: Assessing for Impacts 57
Articulating Different Types of Learning 57
Shifting Our Thinking About Assessment 61
    Qualitative Feedback..............................61
    Specific Feedback 63
Making Impacts Assessable.............................63
    Looking for and Looking at Learning...................64
    Integrating Impacts With Academic Content 65
Simplifying Feedback Practices 69
    Academic Feedback...............................70
    Performance Area Feedback 71
    A Combined Example.............................73
Conclusion..76
Chapter 4 Resources...................................77

Chapter 5
How: Designing Systems Around Impacts 81
Tools and Strategies for Impacts. 82
Implications for Systems. 84
Implications for Learning 88
    Developing a Shared Understanding 88
    Choosing Pathways 89
A Visual Model of the Learning Environment 90
Conclusion. 92
Chapter 5 Resources 93

Chapter 6
How: Facilitating Change 97
Strategic Oversight and Facilitation 98
Preparation for Change 99
    Goal Statements. 100
    Inputs and Outputs. 100
Rolling Strategic Process 103
    Generation. 105
    Execution. 106
    Reflection. 107
Implementation Timeline. 108
    Year 1. 109
    Year 2. 109
    Year 3. 110
    Road-Mapping 110
Two Tracks of Accountability 113
    Did We Do What We Said We Were Going to Do?. 113
    Are We Progressing Toward Achieving Our Mission
        Through Our Impacts?. 114
Conclusion. 118
Chapter 6 Resources 119

Epilogue. 123

Appendix
Sample Performance Areas for Impacts........... 125

References and Resources..................... 129

Index 133

ABOUT THE AUTHOR

Greg Curtis is an author and independent educational consultant. He is based in Beijing, China, and has spent much of his career working with schools around the world in systemwide capacities. Greg has been a technology director, a curriculum and professional learning director, and a strategic planner for international schools in Europe and Asia. He also works with organizations such as EdLeader21, the New England Association of Schools and Colleges, Jay McTighe & Associates Consulting, Mastery Transcript Consortium, and many schools and districts around the world. His work focuses on long-term, systems-based change and strategic transformation around impacts and modern learning in schools and districts. Greg is coauthor of *Learning Personalized: The Evolution of the Contemporary Classroom* (with Allison Zmuda and Diane Ullman), and *Leading Modern Learning: A Blueprint for Vision-Driven Schools* (with Jay McTighe).

He began his teaching career in Canada, receiving his teaching degree at Queen's University in Kingston, Ontario, and his postgraduate degree at the University of Toronto's Ontario Institute for Studies in Education.

To learn more about Greg's work, visit www.gregcurtis-consulting.ca or follow @jgcurtis on Twitter.

To book Greg Curtis for professional development, contact pd@SolutionTree.com.

FOREWORD

By Jay McTighe

My long and varied career in education has included work at the school, district, and state levels. During those years, I've had numerous experiences that make me appreciate the sound advice offered by Greg Curtis in *Moving Beyond Busy*. Here are four of those experiences, examining each level. Do any of these sound familiar?

Experience 1: I began my career as a fifth-grade teacher. I recall the three days before the students arrived in August as an extremely busy period. There was an all-day districtwide staff development session, featuring a welcome by a board member, a talk by the superintendent, and an "inspirational" keynoter. The next day started with a half-day all-staff meeting at our school that included presentations on new district policies, a fire drill, and sales pitches from an insurance salesman and the teachers' credit union. In the afternoon, we had grade-level meetings and, finally, time to set up our classrooms.

I quickly learned that one of the unspoken expectations in my school was the preparation of eye-catching classroom bulletin boards. It turned out that quite a few of my colleagues had spent many hours during the summer break cutting out fancy letters, preparing multicolored borders, and creating elaborate displays. Some teachers enlisted the help of artistically talented former students to assist in the production. My initial idea had been to keep the walls of my classroom blank and then engage my students in helping to design the look and feel of the room. However, I was shamed by the attractive and creative rooms around me and spent much of Labor Day weekend frantically covering boards in colored paper, cut-out letters, and a few posters featuring cute animals with "motivational" sayings.

Experience 2: During my first few years of teaching, the district offered two professional development days each semester. These days were typically held at a high school where all staff would gather in an auditorium for a lecture by a keynote presenter. This general session was followed by dozens of workshops offered throughout the rest of the day by fellow teachers and district staff. Teachers generally enjoyed the workshops since we could choose from a wide variety of topics. While teachers appreciated the choices, there seemed to be no common theme connecting the workshop offerings, and very few of the topical sessions had any follow-up later in the school year.

Experience 3: I worked in a school district that launched a major new initiative at the start of each school year. Veteran educators in the district referred to this phenomenon as T.Y.N.T. (translation—This Year's New Thing). This contrasted with L.Y.N.T. (Last Year's New Thing) and the expected N.Y.N.T. While these various annual initiatives were well-intentioned, the level of explanation, professional development, and follow-through was generally insufficient to ensure much chance of successful implementation. Moreover, there was rarely any discussion of how these various initiatives worked together to achieve impacts on student learning.

When I moved from the school level to a position in the district office, I became aware that the selection of each annual initiative seemed to be based on whatever new book the superintendent had read or the latest conference he attended. Not surprisingly, the pattern of adding initiatives each year resulted in a "this-too-shall-pass" attitude that kept many teachers and administrators from fully investing in any particular initiative because, predictably, the district would shift its focus to something else the following year.

Experience 4: For a portion of my career, I worked in a state department of education in the division of instruction. The assistant superintendent who headed the division held bimonthly meetings on Monday mornings, and all staff were expected to attend. The purposes of the meetings were not always clear, and there were rarely any outputs as a result. Nonetheless, attendance was taken and staff could find themselves in the dog house if they were absent without approved leave or a doctor's note. While there were often more pressing matters reflecting departmental priorities, these meetings consumed four to six hours each month.

These four cases—and many others that I could cite—illustrate examples of:

- Working hard, but not smart
- A focus on inputs and compliance rather than outcomes
- An emphasis on activities and products rather than results
- Lack of clear, long-term goals followed by a systemic plan to achieve them
- Failure to connect various initiatives in support of a well-articulated impact on student learning
- Poor allocations of time and energy

Thankfully, Greg Curtis offers practical and proven advice to help avert these familiar flaws in educational operations. His I-O-I framework importantly distinguishes inputs (such as plans and expenditures) and outputs (products such as a workshop series or a new reporting system) from impacts—demonstrable effects on student learning. He describes the power of backward design to align actions and work synergistically toward worthy, long-term achievements for learners. As the book's title suggests, he reminds us that being busy or working vigorously does not necessarily result in effective and lasting change in the performance of students.

According to the I-O-I framework, reading this book would be considered an input. I believe that the potential impact on your practice will be well worth it!

INTRODUCTION

In schools and districts around the world, K–12 leaders invariably hear educators say, "This is the busiest place I've ever worked!" And by and large, this statement is not hyperbolic; their harried feeling is true to the incredible busyness we experience working at 21st century schools. But do schools and districts keep teachers and leaders busy doing the right work?

Programmatic change and implementation seem to drive much of this busyness. Schools often introduce initiatives in a way that can only be described as fast and furious. Educators scramble to keep up with all the change, let alone make meaningful shifts that create a lasting difference. In many schools, numerous initiatives and programs like STEM, STEAM, 21st century learning, and cultural responsiveness fight for attention and obscure each other, leaving teachers unsure where to focus their efforts. Rather than an integrative environment centered on a small number of clear, connected, and important student learning goals, the layering of initiatives creates an additive environment. We often hear people say, "I have too much on my plate," conveying that things pile on top of each other instead of cohering into a single effort toward a small set of important goals. This trend toward overbuilt environments, with their layers of unrelated, unfinished initiatives and innovations, can cause educators to work at a hectic pace toward no defined end goal. Often, the back-end focus on shifting implementations and delivery models overtakes the forward-facing work of enhancing student learning.

This frenetic and resource-heavy approach does not serve schools' and districts' transformational goals. Educators have expended a tremendous amount of human capital, but it has not led to the shifts that progressive voices and research say schools need, such as personalized learning, a project approach, or 21st century skills. The problem is deceptively simple: a lack of clear learning goals at the heart of desired transformations means that we are forever tinkering with new approaches and delivery models. This distracts us from a true focus on student learning as envisioned by the school's mission. Without clear, transformative learning goals and metrics for assessing them, schools forever implement untethered innovations. We overload the environment with new fads and initiatives, obscuring the desired learning. We need to break out of this cycle in which many schools find themselves trapped. We need to move from *additive* to *integrative* and jettison any unconnected or distracting practices.

The contents of this book can help leaders of educational organizations develop a powerful focus on transformational learning as the core of their work and the measure of their success. By doing so, educational organizations can also reduce unnecessary busyness and focus their energies on helping students tangibly achieve essential goals for modern learning. To do this, we first need to adopt a framework for effective transformation.

A Framework for Effective Transformation

As school and district leaders, our goal is not to implement the greatest number of new initiatives and programs. Our goal is to first pinpoint the high-level learning goals that prepare our students to face an ambiguous and complex future. Then, we must carefully align new initiatives with these learning goals and rigorously assess initiatives' effectiveness in achieving them.

This focus, combined with a commitment to capturing and interpreting evidence of these transformational learning goals, can drive change throughout connected teaching and learning systems and bring about focused and achievable transformation. This notion of driving change has a close connection to backward design (Wiggins & McTighe, 2005). In backward design approaches, a commitment to building with the end in mind replaces the notion of starting at the beginning. Instead of starting with the inputs of education, we start with the desired goals and pull everything into orbit around these goals. Backward design, when used properly, forces us to make choices and decide on actions with these clear end goals in mind. When we start from the beginning, we simply strike out on a path and often make choices and select initiatives without an informed idea of what we're after. By committing to a few clear and focused end goals, we work to align all the systems that feed into the achievement of these goals in a focused backward design approach.

I call this approach the Input-Output-Impact (I-O-I)® framework. As Jay McTighe and I discuss in *Leading Modern Learning* (2019), I-O-I and backward design are mutually supporting structures. I-O-I adds to backward design by bringing desired transformational learning goals (impacts) alongside organizational actions and products (inputs and outputs) in a new way. It is a very accessible framework of interrelated structures that guide learning change and transformation, and it helps break the cycle of unending and untethered busyness. We will dig into I-O-I in chapter 2 (page 21), but in short:

- *Inputs* are organizational actions and resources, often the action steps of a strategic plan.
- *Outputs* are the results of these actions and commitments of resources, often in the form of programs, structures, and physical spaces.
- *Impacts* are the transformational learning goals at the heart of your mission.

Figure I.1 provides a simple representation of the framework.

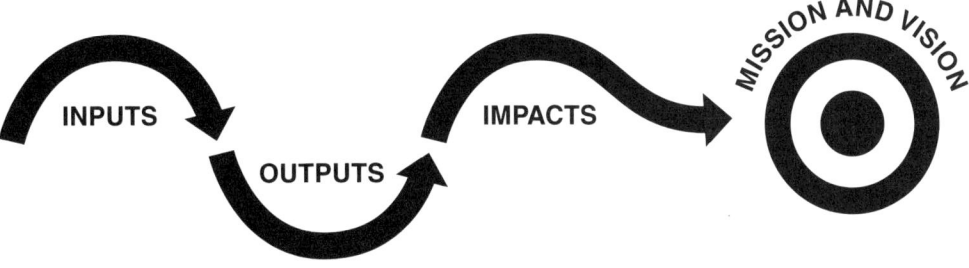

FIGURE I.1: The basics of the Input-Output-Impact framework.

I-O-I bridges the gap between aspirational missions and visions and real learning and teaching. It simplifies the process of achieving transformation through a disciplined backward design framework. In the process, I-O-I gathers all work and learning into a single initiative. The result is tighter alignment between the ends and the means, allowing educators to focus on a few meaningful shifts, rather than graze at a seemingly endless buffet of possible innovations.

The *Why*, *What*, and *How* of Change

In his book *Start With Why: How Great Leaders Inspire Everyone to Take Action*, Simon Sinek (2009) famously posits that when leaders propose a change, they should always start with the *why* behind the change, followed by the *how* and the *what* of the change. This is a form of backward design and, as Sinek (2009) explains, makes good sense for business scenarios. However, while the why is the best place to start, this book posits that schools should reverse the other two layers. Schools are extremely complex organizations that necessitate this reversal. Indeed, placing the how before the what (as in Sinek's structure) is one of the main reasons why schools and districts often flounder in their change efforts. For schools, the sequence should go from why to what to how (see figure I.2).

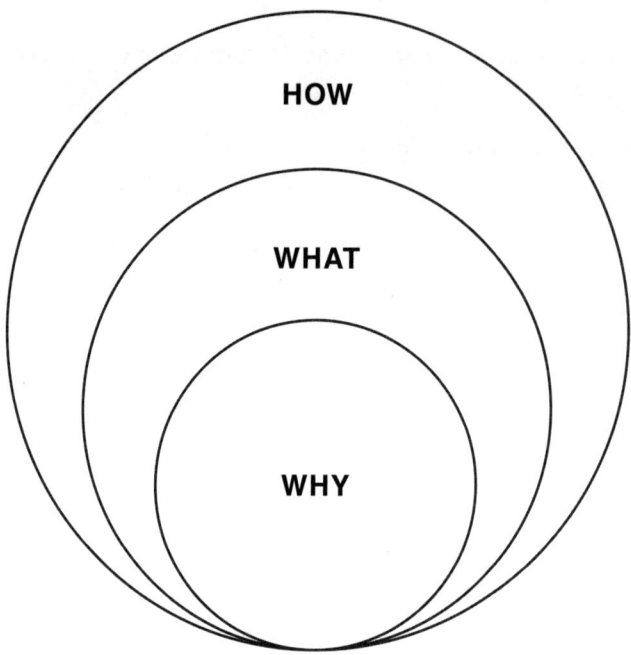

FIGURE I.2: The why-what-how sequence.

Beginning with the why of change is, of course, essential. In much of the work of schools and educational organizations, we need a future-oriented approach that clearly articulates the rationale for why change will prepare students for their futures. The what then articulates our responses to the why. For example, if a reason for change is the fact that students will need to navigate a future of multiple careers that emerge and change frequently, the corresponding what might emphasize self-directed learning as a way to set students up for success in that future. Finally, the how encompasses the strategic work the school will undertake to achieve the what. Unfortunately, many educational organizations skip to the how before establishing the first two layers, thereby contributing to the untethered busyness we want to avoid. Floundering in the how is a sure sign that a school or organization needs to step back to the why and the what. The development of an effective and focused how must be predicated on the clarity of purpose and goals articulated in the why and what. Moving the how to the end of the transformational process is one of this book's main themes.

The Structure of This Book

The structure of this book follows the progression from why to what to how. The book's chapters will help you answer the following questions and take the corresponding actions in your school or district.

- "**Why** do we need to change?" (Consider the flaws of your current processes for identifying and articulating change goals.)
- "**What** might we do instead?" (Use the Input-Output-Impact framework to align your actions with your goals.)
- "**How** do we do it?" (Adjust classroom practices and school systems to support your highest learning goals.)

Chapter 1 focuses on the why. Change efforts over the first decades of the 21st century have not resulted in much tangible progress. We need to face this failure in order to commit to another way of doing things. The chapter explores the question, Why does our current approach to change create so much busyness that does not lead to the deep changes we seek? In other words, why have the traditional ways of approaching change and transformation led to a predictable pattern of failure and systemic exhaustion?

Chapter 2 shows that if our existing way of working *isn't* working, our next step should be to propose a different way to achieve our goals. Therefore, chapter 2 delves into the what with the question, What is the Input-Output-Impact framework, and in what way might we use it to realign our thinking and action so we achieve real and lasting change? Because the input and output elements of the framework will be more familiar to educators, this book focuses mainly on impacts.

Once we have established the why and what, the remaining chapters address various aspects of the how. Chapter 3 considers the question, How might we choose and act on essential learning impacts for our students? Without a clear articulation of our highest goals for learning, we will probably spin in the same circles we always have. In order to act on our mission with direction and focus, we first need to articulate the learning goals at the heart of this mission. In this chapter, we will explore a basic process for choosing impacts and a structure for operationalizing them.

Next, chapter 4 considers the question, How will we know that our intended learning is actually happening? Once we have an articulated set of learning goals (our impacts), how do we assess them? This chapter explores how we may need to shift our views on assessment, how we might bring impacts alongside academic goals in our assessment design, and how we might provide meaningful and quantifiable feedback to students to support this desired learning.

Chapter 5 explores the use of impacts as catalysts for strategic thinking. The central question for this chapter is, How do we focus our strategic thinking and organizational efforts on achieving our impacts? The implications of impacts are both broad and deep. Busyness is scattered; meaningful work is targeted. The ideas and processes discussed in this chapter can ensure that we limit scattered busyness and target our work so it leads to thoughtful and lasting change.

In chapter 6, we ask, How do we structure and evaluate the change process based on I-O-I? Reducing busyness does not mean rejecting the work needed to achieve our mission. We will explore a rolling strategic process as an alternative to flawed traditional strategic plans. We can use I-O-I in conjunction with this adaptive, iterative process to simply yet powerfully develop and act on long-term strategic goals for learning (that is, impacts). We will also deal with some possible approaches to assess and communicate an organization's progress toward achieving its mission through impacts.

Each chapter ends with a series of questions and suggested activities to engage readers and school teams in collaborative learning.

This book also features recurring Stop! sections. These sections list the unrelated, untethered things we should stop doing in order to prioritize the new, future-focused work. We cannot do everything we currently do *and* the new processes outlined in this book. We must stop doing some things in order to focus on the challenging work ahead. Identifying what we should stop doing is an important part of choosing work that is aligned and mutually supportive.

The Goal of This Book

The goal of this book is to introduce the I-O-I framework, its implications, and its potential to support meaningful change as an alternative to a stream of unrelated implementations. Each chapter will share structures, processes, and examples to support leaders' activation of this approach. Enacting the I-O-I framework will take a large scope of work that involves:

- Identifying core transformational learning goals
- Operationalizing these goals through a straightforward planning and change implementation process
- Using resulting evidence and data to assess the level to which organizational efforts are achieving the mission and vision and the transformational goals embodied therein

It is still hard work, but I-O-I is focused and targeted on progress toward meaningful learning and can lessen the frenetic busyness often found within learning organizations. It turns our eyes toward quality rather than quantity. The transformation comes through the depth of the shifts we make and the achievement of the desired student learning, not the number of changes we implement.

This book will interest district and school leaders who want a guide for reframing change efforts in their organizations. However, it also features many elements that coaches, teacher leaders, and teachers themselves will find of interest. This book rests on the premise that a shift like the I-O-I framework can produce major changes for learning and how we work within schools, departments, and classrooms. While the primary audience is K–12 educators, the premise can also apply in higher education and the general nonprofit sector. This book should prove useful for book groups and as a common reading for appropriate teams.

It is essential that a single leader or small group not read this book and introduce it as an initiative or program for the rest of the organization in a top-down manner. This runs counter to the foundational why-what-how premise and is a key mistake schools commit on a regular basis. The broad shifts outlined in this book affect all systems within schools and will require effective change management and leadership. Please use this book as a catalyst for these efforts.

CHAPTER 1

WHY

Identifying Problems With the Traditional Approach to Change

This first chapter will make the case for changing our approach to school improvement and transformation. Our traditional way of operating, at a strategic level, has not had a significant positive effect on learning. That is a bold statement, but it's true in the vast majority of cases. Educators may have shifted some ways in which teaching and learning take place, but goals for learning and for designing change have largely remained the same. To put it simply, we may have updated some of our approaches, but our learning goals have not changed markedly (have a look at a report card, and you will not find new learning goals that weren't there at the beginning of this century). The efforts that have gone into change initiatives have not, by and large, been commensurate with the expectations of real change in the classroom. We have been very busy, but the effects are often underwhelming.

Anyone proposing a change in how learning organizations function must first establish the premise that change is necessary. As articulated in the introduction, this chapter's central question is, Why does our current approach to change create so much busyness that does not lead to the deep changes we seek? We shouldn't simply change because we *want* to; we should change because we *need* to in order to achieve the meaningful and necessary shifts in learning that our students deserve.

Schools are very busy places. They are complex environments made more complicated by a myriad of trend-chasing initiatives. But we should not confuse busyness with progress. In fact, busyness is often the enemy of purposeful progress. According to an Education Week Research Center online survey, which samples a nationally representative group of more than five hundred K–12 teachers in the United States, "There are signs teachers are starting to feel reform fatigue: More than half of teachers (58 percent) surveyed said they've experienced 'way too much' or 'too much' change in the last couple of years" (Loewus, 2017). School and district leadership also faces a large number of compliance tasks that add to stress and limit the ability to tend to mission-driven change efforts. One middle school principal states that he spends "80 percent of his days just making sure the school is in compliance with city education mandates" (Collette, 2015). He adds, "They're so worked up about compliance issues and deadlines instead of me being the instructional leader for the school" (Collette, 2015).

To add to the sense of futility that many teachers and leaders feel, they often sense that busyness is cyclical, swinging back and forth between various reforms and initiatives:

> Educational movements are like pendulum swings, traveling with an irresistible thrust; then, unheralded, a new campaign drives yet another educational cause back the other direction, gaining momentum. Each new crusade, at first invincible, soon succumbs and is superseded by an opposing force just as powerful and relentless as its predecessors, until it too is supplanted with a new fervid impulsion. (Page, 2002)

This is not to say that busyness and change are the root of all stress in schools. Teaching and educational leadership are demanding professions, often leading to stress. It is also not to say that we should reduce stress by simply eliminating all efforts to change teaching and learning. Schools should always have change initiatives in play as teaching and learning must continue to evolve. However, the negative effect of the busyness in schools is largely self-inflicted (by the institution, not the individuals) through too many unfocused, unconnected, and unclear initiatives.

Educators and policymakers used to talk about teacher burnout as the outcome of such workplace stress. However, Doris A. Santoro (2018) has made the case for an alternative manifestation: demoralization. As Santoro (2018) explains, "The diagnosis of demoralization characterizes the problem as a value conflict experienced as a result of policies, mandates, and school practices." This value conflict often strikes some of the most dedicated teachers as their work drifts further and further from the reasons they entered the profession. Brave and committed individuals will champion change for their students' benefit, but many become demoralized when the benefits are not achieved or don't stick. When your strongest resources—committed teachers—give up, you lose valuable voices and resources. We must reduce the stress and demoralization associated with change by making the transformations we seek meaningful, targeted, achievable, and sustainable. To set the stage for a more productive approach to change, the remainder of this chapter explores the problems with our traditional approaches to change implementation, missions and visions, and strategic plans.

The Problem With Change Implementation

Why do most change efforts fail to bring about meaningful change? It's not that educators aren't trying. Schools and districts commit significant resources to change efforts—time, personnel, and funds—yet these efforts rarely have the desired effect on teaching and learning. Many learning organizations have become implementation factories, chasing new approaches and fads and searching for that silver bullet that will finally transform the ways we teach and learn.

Take the attempt to use technology to transform schools as an example. Beginning in the 1990s, many leaders and educators, myself included, believed that technology would change everything. Now, in 2019, I find that we are still waiting (though perhaps the changes are still to come). Why? Teachers have busily tried to implement technology, but without well-articulated goals for what all this work is supposed to accomplish. Much new technology has been focused on professional tasks (curriculum mapping, reporting systems, class websites, and so on), while others focus on the presentation and delivery of content. These approaches often put the how before the what and assume that everyone shares the same understanding of the why. The emphasis is frequently placed on using more technology more often. While technology has changed much of how we work (largely on the administrative side), the potential shifts in student learning, for the most part, have not been achieved. This fixation on implementation tends to result in change bouncing off the resilient shell of complex ecosystems like schools. We cannot hope that these innovations alone will drive transformation if we do not modernize our goals for student learning in a very real way. These modern goals for learning are represented by what I call *impacts*.

We must stop:
- Looking at implementation as a goal in and of itself
- Unwittingly subscribing to the "more is better" view of school change
- Looking at innovations as silver bullets, able to fix everything on their own
- Mistaking modernizing learning for implementing the latest fad or approach

The Problem With Missions and Visions

A fascinating dichotomy often exists between what a school says it values through its mission and vision and what learning goals it attends to on a daily basis. It's as if the two exist in different spheres and for different purposes. A cynic might go so far as to say that mission and vision statements exist to compartmentalize ideals while we go about the "real life" work of teaching and learning. We point to these statements, nod in agreement, even believe in them, and then turn around and do what we've always done. To illustrate this metaphorically, consider the version of the famous cultural iceberg in figure 1.1. While we talk about our mission and vision a great deal, most energy is spent on the day-to-day actions—often there is a misalignment between them.

One need only look at most report cards to see the discrepancy between stated ideals and actual practices. How many report cards have you seen that truly put critical thinking or another 21st century skill on par with, for example, the number or letter grade for mathematics? For curriculum design, the situation is

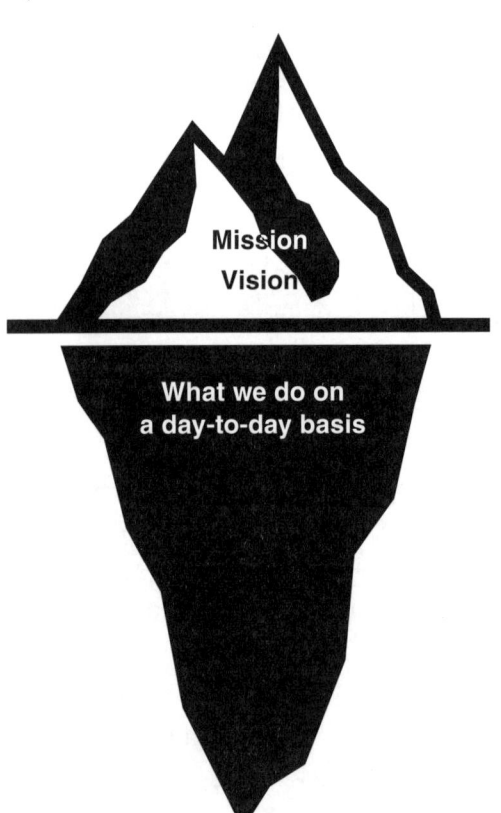

FIGURE 1.1: The mission–practice iceberg.

similar. We say we want to help develop 21st century learners, yet much of our curriculum remains decidedly 20th century. We say we value empathy and resilience, yet we include no place for these skills in our assessment or reporting structures. This discrepancy will probably not surprise anyone. Wishing something were so through a mission or vision statement is not the same as making it so for students.

Often this discrepancy begins with mission and vision statements themselves. For example, take this one: "Strengthen student engagement and learning outcomes by enhancing student support and intervention services" (Barr, 2010). This is a prime example of a statement that includes inert language and *weasel words*—vague terms that we can't observe, touch, or demonstrate, such as "strengthen student engagement." Mission statements are often full of inert language. It's no wonder educators have trouble enacting and measuring their missions. "If people don't share a single, sharply focused, easily imaginable vision of a result they want to create, any effort to measure that result will waste time" (Barr, 2004).

It is fairly easy to determine the degree to which your school has operationalized its mission or vision. Ask two simple questions: (1) "What does our mission or vision look like in practice?" and (2) "How do we know that we're achieving it?" (Curtis, 2018). Few organizations can answer the first question, and the vast majority cannot draw on concrete evidence to address the second. This is often where the difficult but necessary conversation about addressing the discrepancy begins. Mission and vision statements are important, but even more essential is the evidence of student learning aligned to those ideals. As an example, imagine a school that claims to be addressing its mission-centered goal of global citizenship because it has implemented a program and graduation requirements for service learning. This is fantastic, but the school has to ask, "How do we know that this program is achieving our goal of supporting students in becoming global citizens? And, by the way, what does global citizenship look like? What skills and dispositions can students demonstrate to provide evidence that they are achieving this goal? How do we gather evidence that students are developing in these areas?" Without the sort of clarity that comes from this sort of purposeful articulation, we run the risk of running off in different directions without a clear, common set of measurable goals.

As another example, many schools make 21st century learning part of their visions and then implement one-to-one technology programs. Another common goal is creating responsible members of society through a character education program. Having one-to-one devices does not automatically equate with developing 21st century learners. Having a character education program does not result in students suddenly becoming responsible when they finish the program's last worksheet. If operationalizing our missions were that easy and directly causal, we'd have solved many issues long ago. These programs are not evidence of the schools' achieving mission-driven goals; they merely represent evidence of the schools' implementing a program. These cases exemplify schools conflating ends and means (Curtis, 2018).

Most schools have organizational aspirations to improve learning so that they can address their students' real and urgent needs. Mission and vision statements are full of such noble aspirations as global citizenship, 21st century learning, or the ability to thrive in an ever-changing future. We still have these aspirations in spite of the compliance requirements and standardized tasks schools and districts face via federal, state, and local mandates and reforms. These aspirations are meaningful; however, schools often set them aside in favor of traditional goals and metrics for learning. Schools and districts are distracted from these aspirations by accountability requirements that ask for little more than a test score. An alignment between the aspirations in the mission and what day-to-day actions strive toward is essential to achieving these noble goals.

The Problem With Strategic Plans

One need only look at the traditional, static strategic planning process to see why much of this ineffective busyness has come to be. From the beginning, this planning process often gets sidetracked:

> Often, people get lost in the semantics of defining their vision, mission and values. They spend so much time and effort trying to understand what those terms mean and how they fit together that by the time they have it all figured out, they're mentally fatigued. As a consequence, once they get to the actual plan creation and implementation, they're just trying to get it done and over with. Their energy is drained and now they're in survival mode, which is never a good mind-set for strategic planning. (Price, n.d.)

Even if the planning process results in a plan document, most strategic plans are full of questionable actions and implementations. Aside from the inappropriateness of long-term, fixed strategic plan documents, they present flawed thinking in an era where nothing is fixed or static. They list what we will do, but often neglect to mention what we want to *achieve* through this effort and expenditure of human and financial resources. Worse, the strategies may focus on what is easiest or most practical for the organization, instead of what would most benefit students. And thus the strategic plan becomes a gerbil wheel, never leading to any learning progress (see figure 1.2).

Why: Identifying Problems With the Traditional Approach to Change 15

M.C. Escher's Gerbils

© 2010 by Ted Nunes. Reproduction rights obtained from www.CartoonStock.com.

FIGURE 1.2: The gerbil wheel of school strategic plans.

For example, a school might write a strategic plan to establish makerspaces by listing the process and resources it needs to do so. But makerspaces are not a goal—they are a vehicle to achieve a goal. The goal is not simply the implementation of something. Our goal is the learning we seek, such as skill in design processes, innovation, and the like. Do we have evidence that the makerspace is helping to achieve these goals? Are we teaching and assessing these things?

Judging the success of school transformation requires a shift in thinking. Often, we carefully track the achievement of all the actions and implementations contained in a static strategic plan. If the plan said we should create a makerspace and we did, we say we were successful. If we followed the plan and checked all the boxes, we're done. However, checking off actions measures only the plan's implementation, not its effects. Again, it focuses on organizational actions instead of student learning. In other words, we measure the wrong things. Would a factory assess its goal of improving efficiency simply by stating that it implemented the new robotics program? No, it would measure its success based on its efficiency statistics and the level to which the new robotics program contributed to this improvement or lack thereof. Would a restaurant say it has achieved its mission because it published a new menu? A restaurant, depending on its mission, might instead look at metrics like high customer satisfaction and repeat business as a result of its innovative use of local ingredients. A menu is a vehicle, not a goal. While schools should not necessarily emulate factories or restaurants, the examples clarify the issue. The hard-to-measure elements of their missions and visions often challenge schools:

> Unfortunately, there is often a disconnect between whether something can be measured and whether it should be measured. Therefore, one of the biggest mistakes that people make with [goals] is measuring everything that is easy to measure, regardless of its relevance. (Marr, n.d.)

However, just because it is hard doesn't mean we should shrink from the challenge. We should not avoid assessing these goals simply because there are no standardized tests for them and they require different thinking and metrics.

In order to lead to transformation, a plan needs to center on clear, transformational strategic goals instead of the usual operational goals. Operational goals often involve quality control, attention to long-standing or self-contained programs, or the organization's general functioning. Transformational goals are, quite simply, directed toward the achievement of the organization's or department's mission and vision. Of course, operational activities support progress toward a strategic goal, but operation is not a goal in and of itself; it is a vehicle to reach the goal of achieving the mission and vision.

Table 1.1 contains some sample goals that illustrate the distinctions between these two types of goals. A template is provided at the end of the chapter in the "Chapter 1 Resources" reproducible (page 18).

Table 1.1: Examples of Operational Goals Versus Transformational Strategic Goals

Operational Goals	Transformational Strategic Goals
• Establishing strategies for financial stability • Implementing a new reading program • Upgrading a facility • Increasing regular attendance • Improving the school's ranking within the state	• Developing critical, creative, and adaptive thinkers • Developing self-directed learners with high levels of agency and self-efficacy • Developing empathetic learners and citizens who act on their understanding of the perspectives of others

In the coming chapters of the book, we will explore ways to get off the gerbil wheel and make progress toward our transformational goals.

>
> We must stop:
> - Focusing on long lists of actions stretching into the distant future
> - Overloading strategic plans with things that are not actually strategic
> - Spreading valuable resources and energy thinly across initiatives that are not clearly related to transformational strategic goals
> - Mindlessly following a static strategic plan that was written years ago and has never been updated
> - Mistaking busyness for progress

Conclusion

We cannot measure the level to which we are achieving our mission by how tired we feel at the end of the day, week, month, or school year. If leaders get too busy with the how of change, they will lose sight of the why and the what, leading to unproductive busyness. Mission and vision statements may describe our aspirations and our well-meaning desire to do what's best for students, but these statements often remain separate from what we do because they are not anchored in clear, achievable, and assessable goals for learning. Strategic plans are often full of vague statements followed by arduous sets of actions that don't seem to lead anywhere different or meaningful. Educators traditionally measure progress through evidence of implementation rather than evidence of progress toward essential learning goals. All of this generates cycles of intense but untethered and unaccountable activity. As a result, missions remain unrealized. It can also exhaust the systems and the hardworking people within them. Change fatigue, demoralization, and cynicism often result from unrealized or unsustainable change efforts.

Doing what we've always done and hoping for new results wastes energy, resources, and promise. Without goal clarity and a commitment to achieve the goals within a mission or vision, we will not move from aspirational to intentional and toward the changes we seek for our students. Having established why we need change, we will explore what we can do instead in the next chapter.

Chapter 1 Resources

School and district teams can use the following questions and activities to put the concepts from this chapter into action. Teams should retain artifacts resulting from these exercises to inform later work.

Collaborative Inquiry

Consider the following questions, then discuss your answers as a team.

- What are our goals, beyond completing the actions in the strategic plan or our yearly plan?
- Do we have an example of when the existing change process has led to substantive change or improvement? Do we have an example of when it hasn't?
- How do we measure the success of our actions?
- How much of your day is focused on the achievement of our mission?
- How do your colleagues typically react to a report on a strategic plan or the introduction of coming plans and initiatives?

Collaborative Activities

The following activities will help you and your team operationalize the ideas from this chapter. Each activity builds on the one before it, so we recommend completing them in the order shown. Be sure to review the instructions in advance and gather any needed materials, such as markers and chart paper.

Word Salad

Look at your school or district's core documents, and extract all the statements about values, mission, vision, learning principles, and so on. Put them all on a slide or piece of poster paper. Engage in dialogue on some basic questions such as:

- What are we trying to say with all these words?
- What is the connection between all these statements?
- How much of this text is focused on the organization, and how much is focused on students and learning?
- When scanning all these words and statements, how might we answer the question, "What do all of these words mean in terms of our goals for student learning?"

Language Activation

In this chapter, we discussed that the inert nature of language in most mission, vision, and value statements is an impediment to tangibly understanding their desired end. Take some inert language or weasel words from your Word Salad inquiry, and try changing some of this inert language into more concrete sensory language or "language that moves us":

> This "language that moves us" is often comprised of sensory based language, because it describes the experiences we have through our physical senses: what we would see, hear, feel or do, taste or smell if that result were occurring. . . . So if a goal or result is to be measurable, then it must be able to be described in terms of what someone would see, hear, feel or do, taste or smell if that result were occurring. (Barr, n.d., p. 6)

What has changed with this change of language?

Missed Opportunities

Send a random curriculum unit or even a single assessment design to your team before you meet. Ask people to simply read this before meeting. After you have completed the Word Salad exercise, bring out the unit or assessment, and engage in dialogue on these simple questions.

- Which of the goals discussed in our Word Salad inquiry are explicit within this sample curriculum or assessment?
- Do we have missed opportunities to elevate these goals and explicitly include them in curriculum or assessment? What might those be?

Mission Walk

Individually or in pairs, go for a walk through the hallways of your school. Take pictures of things that you believe represent the achievement of your mission and vision (student work on display, highlights of school news, posters for upcoming events, the trophy case, and so on). Return to the group, and share some of these examples. Engage in dialogue on some basic questions such as:

- How does this piece of evidence represent the achievement of our mission and vision for learning?
- Did it result from purposeful actions we took, or have we interpreted it and retrofitted it to our mission?
- Do we provide feedback to our students on the mission-driven goals for learning represented here?
- How might we interpret the level to which it demonstrates elements of our mission? What might evidence of a higher level of alignment look like? A lower one? How might we differentiate the level of quality?
- What other evidence might we collect, and how might we interpret it?
- How might we answer the question, How do we know that we are achieving our mission and vision?

Goal-Setting Template

Our Operational Goals	Our Transformational Strategic Goals

CHAPTER 2

WHAT
Realigning Thought and Action

Chapter 1 established why we need change and why the way we have been pursuing transformation does not suit modern learning. This chapter will succinctly explain the what of change by outlining a framework that will help educators achieve that change. Specifically, this chapter answers the question, What is the Input-Output-Impact framework, and in what way might we use it to realign our thinking and action so we achieve real and lasting change? We'll discuss the details of the framework and explore how I-O-I supports planning and implementation.

Defining Input-Output-Impact

As previously stated, educators have expended a great deal of well-intentioned blood, sweat, and tears in pursuit of the change students need in order to face their future equipped and confident. These efforts have led to some collateral change. However, they have rarely caused the deeper shifts that are essential to achieving the goal of education that reflects future (and even current) realities. This goal must be at the center of all endeavors within a school. This is how we create alignment with our purpose. Instead of pushing transformation through the implementation of programs, educators must pull all activities and systems into alignment with that central commitment. This is the heart of the Input-Output-Impact framework.

The introduction included a simple graphic representing the structure and relationships between inputs, outputs, and impacts (figure I.1, page 3). A more operational representation appears in figure 2.1. It is a fairly simple framework. Inputs and outputs reflect the work a school does. Impacts, however, represent the core transformational goals for learning in a school or district. The I-O-I framework guides backward design for planning and forward implementation for enacting the plan in a more linear fashion.

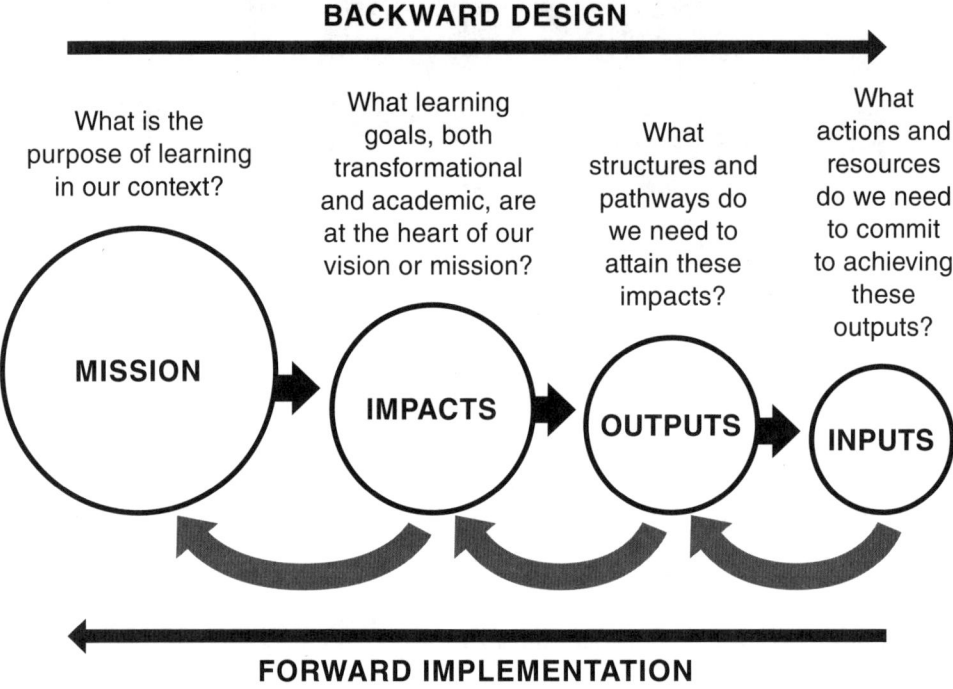

FIGURE 2.1: The Input-Output-Impact framework.

The following text further defines impacts, outputs, and inputs.

Impacts

Since impacts differ from standard academic learning goals, they require a different identifier. In our everyday language, the word *impact* simply means "effect." In the context of I-O-I, *impact* means the desired transformations we seek for our students. These transformational goals go beyond simple learning targets, standards, content, or procedural knowledge. They are the things we highlight in our missions and visions yet rarely address in any real or purposeful way. The disconnect between mere activity and demonstrable success often arises because of the lack of clear learning goals at the heart of a school's mission and vision—the impacts. To further clarify, consider the following descriptors (Curtis, 2018).

- An impact represents the highest goals for student learning, often spanning academic areas.
- An impact should strive for a transformative goal, not a traditional cumulative learning goal in traditional subject areas.
- An impact should represent a moral imperative or "moral purpose" (Fullan, 2002) for the organization.
- An impact should clarify how schooling will be designed to meet the challenges and opportunities of our students' futures.
- An impact must be student centered, not organization centered.
- An impact must be compelling and understandable to the broader community.
- An impact must be learnable and demonstrable so educators can regularly observe and capture students' demonstrations of the skills and dispositions related to it.

In a nutshell, impacts are the things that will help students become the best versions of themselves, beyond what they know within a subject area. While they transcend academic content, they are still learnable and demonstrable. Impacts are simple and often familiar. In many ways, they've been around for a long, long time. Mission and vision statements are full of them, although we often leave impacts unrealized or unarticulated. We see examples of these in vague statements such as *prepared for a changing world*, *a responsible citizen of the world*, and other phrases that sound nice, but lack specific, tangible learning goals.

What is new and different is not the words but what we do with them. The following are some examples of impacts.

- Global citizenship
- Leadership
- Systems thinking
- Creativity
- Collaboration
- Flexible thinking
- Empathy
- Problem solving
- Resilience
- Civic participation
- Self-directed learning

These skills and dispositions represent much of what lies at the core of missions and visions. As described in chapter 1 (page 12), these ideals often remain confined to idle statements while we continue with our traditional business of teaching and learning. However, when coupled with a commitment to focusing curriculum, assessment, grading, and reporting on evidence of student learning in impact areas (in addition to academic goals), they can create a powerful shift.

Outputs

Outputs are the things produced through, or as a result of organizational activity. Most strategic plans are targeted at producing outputs, such as new programs, physical spaces, policies, and so on. Outputs are important, but (as previously stated) they usually represent the logical conclusion of a series of actions or use of resources (see Inputs). These are categorically different from impacts, which, quite simply, are the transformational learning goals at the heart of an organization's mission. In short, outputs are the products of the things an organization does (inputs). They may produce evidence of achievement of impacts, but they are not impacts in and of themselves.

Inputs

Inputs are the actions and resources committed by the organization to the achievement of outputs. For example, we may commit professional learning time and money to support the development of a service learning program (an output). We may commit funds and human resources to the development of new learning spaces. These are, obviously, important to school change efforts. However, in and of themselves, they do not represent the achievement of impacts. We can assess the level to which inputs and outputs (our strategies) have helped move student learning toward achievement of impacts, but simply completing steps in a plan is not the same as evidence of impacts derived from student learning.

Supporting Planning With I-O-I

The I-O-I framework guides schools in planning for change, from transformational goals down to specific actions. Clearly articulating and unpacking a few impacts can guide the development and alignment of all systems within a school or district. This shift occurs through a concerted effort to achieve these impacts and to assess that achievement through evidence of student learning. It is challenging but provides a powerful sense of focus for all members of a school community.

Figure 2.2 illustrates the components of I-O-I for supporting an example impact, or goal, of self-directed learning. The framework simply gives us a way to break down the work by planning backward from the learning goal. In a real-life setting, we would usually accompany such a planning grid with time frames and lists of who is responsible for each input, resources needed, and so forth. A reproducible template that includes all these factors appears at the end of this chapter (page 35).

IMPACT	
Self-directed learning: Improve student self-direction through an evidence-based goal-setting process.	
Outputs	**Inputs**
Develop a guided inquiry approach to goal setting.	• Gather a small design team of teachers. • Research samples of goal-setting structures. • Devise steps and prompts for student-guided inquiry into students' learning evidence and resulting goal setting. • Develop concise documentation to assist students and teachers in going through the process. • Prototype the goal-setting approach, refine, and submit for feedback. • Get approval from leadership team.
Design and develop a digital interface to support the student goal-setting process within a digital dashboard system.	• Gather a small team of teachers and students. • Develop a storyboard to illustrate the steps in the process. • Provide designs to developers so they can create a wireframe. • Upon completion, prototype the wireframe, gather and organize feedback into requests for revision, and submit them to designers and developers. • Review and sign off on the revisions.
Implement a goal-setting process and module for the identified grade levels.	• Develop communication and orientation plans. • Introduce the why and what of the initiative across the community. • Engage teachers and leaders in orientation sessions. • Engage students in orientation sessions. • Roll out the goal-setting process and module. • Collect evidence, and assess the level to which this process supported student growth in the desired impact.

FIGURE 2.2: Planning for the Input-Output-Impact framework.

We may measure inputs and outputs by the completion of action steps and implementation plans. The achievement of desired impacts, however, should be evidenced through the artifacts and products of student learning. The measure of success is not that we did the work, but that students learned and can demonstrate their growth and achievement related to stated impacts. For example, students may produce evidence demonstrating the achievement of goals for self-directed learning or growth mindset through successful and meaningful engagement in the goal-setting process. We also require appropriate metrics to assess student performance and growth in these areas—new metrics for new learning goals. We cannot interpret modern learning with a set of assessment tools built largely for the 20th century. Specific metrics, designed to provide qualitative feedback on evidence of impacts, will be more fully explored in chapter 4.

Driving Action With I-O-I

Once we have a plan in place, I-O-I also supports implementation by prioritizing flexible, iterative progress and keeping the end goal in mind. To make a comparison to the business world, impacts play a role similar to key performance indicators (KPIs). While we do not seek to mimic that environment, the notion of identifying indicators against which we assess our progress is equally valid in education. In business, KPIs are largely quantifiable measures, such as the number of new contracts signed per period, revenue growth, or percentage of market share (Enochson, n.d.). A business would continually assess progress toward these end goals. In education, the indicators are your impacts—the long-term, clearly articulated, and demonstrable learning goals at the heart of your organization's mission and vision. As such, school leaders should frequently assess and make adjustments based on the school's progress toward achieving its impacts.

As described previously (see chapter 1, page 14), traditional, fixed-term strategic plans are not appropriate to the challenges and realities we face in education. Many strategic plans fail because they are not iterative or agile enough to take advantage of new learning or to react to emergent opportunities or challenges. In the 21st century, we cannot pretend that we can predict the future:

> Traditional strategic planning was based on the assumption that one could measure all of the variables that were relevant to the future of a business, analyze the results, and construct strategies based upon the results that, if followed, would ensure future success. However, even the best strategies experience unforeseen economic, industry, social, and market shifts. The fallacy

of prediction inevitably led to the downfall of traditional strategic planning, because the strategies could not deliver what they promised: predictable success. (Mendenhall & Pryor, n.d.)

Not only is prediction a fallacy that can lead to failure, but it ignores the fact that strategic thinking should be ongoing and driven largely by insights gained during the process. To remain flexible, "smart leaders constantly have their ear to the ground, listening to threats and opportunities and moving quickly to adjust plans accordingly. Your strategy should be no different" (Wright, 2015).

A rolling strategic process—in contrast to a static plan—seeks to design, prototype, and learn the best ways to address impacts as time passes. In the I-O-I version of the rolling strategic process, which chapter 6 (page 97) will describe more fully, the impacts remain stable while the inputs and outputs are shorter term so that we can refine them with agility. Figure 2.3 illustrates how numerous short-term inputs and outputs contribute to the focused set of long-term impacts. We need to invest in long-term goals in a way that allows us to adjust over time and within changing contexts.

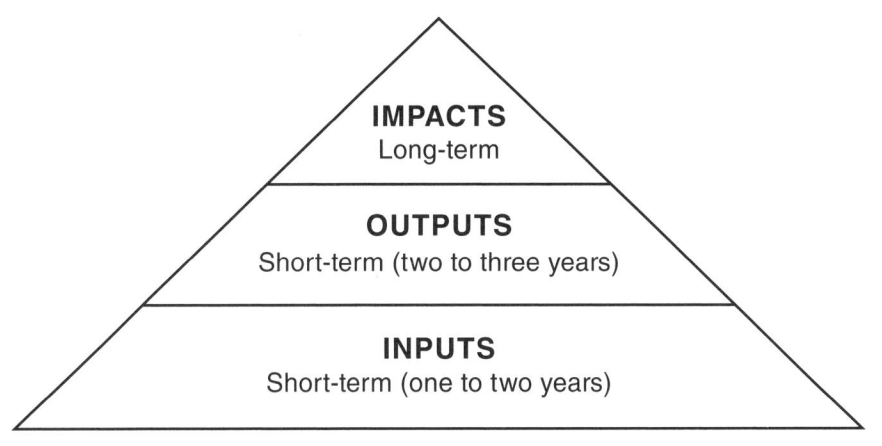

FIGURE 2.3: Long-term and short-term goals.

I-O-I drives change and transformation backward through all the systems within a school. The commitment to defining impacts and measuring success against those goals has implications for all systems within a learning organization. Educators must design and implement assessment, grading, reporting, instruction, professional learning, and every other system to be aligned with the impacts and to provide evidence of progress. As such, I-O-I drives short-term and long-term action throughout the school. Not only does I-O-I become the bridge between our mission and what keeps us busy on a daily basis, but when we hold ourselves accountable to impacts, transformation is the desired result.

Schools are complex organizations, within which multiple systems interact and new properties can emerge—not at random but sometimes unpredictably. Causal relationships are not the norm in complex environments. We can never assume clean causal relationships in schools. We can't say that A will result in B, or that X and Y will ensure that Z happens—for example, we can't say that having a service-learning program will automatically create global citizens. In order to achieve something in complex environments, leaders often need to "tilt" the environment—adaptively nudge it in the right direction without assuming causal relationships—so that the desired outcome emerges. Traditional environments push change; complex environments require a more nuanced approach to adaptive change. This outcome may be transformational for the organization. Much of my approach to transformational and adaptive change is derived from my fascination with complexity theory. I will avoid going too deeply into this area here, but heartily invite leaders to engage in this topic; a list of recommend resources is available at **go.SolutionTree.com/leadership**.

It is for these exact reasons that the I-O-I framework has such potential for transforming schools: I-O-I provides a way to tilt school and district environments so that focused transformations emerge. Most schools genuinely desire the transformational goals they allude to in their missions, but very, very few move from aspirational to intentional. Actualizing the mission requires aligning curriculum, assessment, grading, and reporting systems with the highest goals for learning—not an easy task, but a necessary one.

The I-O-I framework helps us bring the lofty ambitions of missions and visions down to a level that teachers and students can actually engage with. In practice, we do this by developing aligned strategic actions and products—inputs and outputs—needed to achieve our impacts. Finally, evaluating evidence of impacts gives schools the best way to demonstrate the correlation between the undertaken inputs and outputs and the realized learning impacts and achieved mission. In the following sections, we will explore examples of organizations that have used I-O-I to drive action. These examples share a simple premise: I-O-I shifts the way we approach change and provides clarity and a scaffold for acting on powerful intentions.

We must stop:

- Creating long-term, fixed strategic plans that we pretend can predict what the right thing to do will be in, say, five years
- Creating strategic plans that confuse outputs with the true goals—impacts
- Believing that inputs, outputs, and the achievement of impacts have a simple causal relationship (that if we simply do what we say we will do, the desired results will occur)
- Using metrics that are not related to our impacts to measure success
- Thinking of strategic planning as something that we do every few years, rather than taking an ongoing, agile, and involved approach to thinking and acting

School District of Greenfield

The School District of Greenfield in Greenfield, Wisconsin, is a good example of an organization that had realized (largely through community involvement) that it needed to move beyond traditional learning goals. It had identified a number of learning goals that its community believed students needed for their futures. When I started working with Greenfield in 2016, the district asked me, "Now what do we do?" This is typical of many organizations I work with. District leadership (the superintendent and directors of elementary and secondary education) knew the why and had a good start on the what. As superintendent Lisa Elliott describes, "The laser-like focus on student learning and essential student outcomes is what drew us to the I-O-I framework. The concepts of impacts gave us the blueprint to clearly articulate the path we would take" (L. Elliott, personal communication, July 9, 2018).

We used I-O-I to help gain operational clarity on the district's transformational goals for learning before the district jumped to the how. District leadership quickly embraced the notion of impacts as the true measure of success. In fact, through their extensive work with the community, Greenfield had already articulated a number of impacts—Greenfield21 (G21). We used methodologies and frameworks (see chapter 3, page 39) to help operationalize their G21 impacts, focus the work ahead, and shine a light on the need to evidence these impacts through learning, not just the organizational efforts.

First, we streamlined this original long list to a set of seven G21 impacts, illustrated in the student-created graphic in figure 2.4. We then followed many of the structures and processes outlined in chapter 3 (page 39) to help us bring these into the daily learning environment in tangible and demonstrable ways. Patrice Ball, Greenfield's director of secondary education, explains that "the I-O-I framework, along with structured activities, helped us stretch our thinking and helped us visualize student success. Now it seems so very apparent, but at the time it did brush against the traditional system of school and district improvement planning" (P. Ball, personal communication, July 8, 2018).

1. Self-directed learning
2. Creativity
3. Critical thinking
4. Global competence
5. Well-being
6. Collaboration
7. Communication

Source: © 2016 by School District of Greenfield. Created by Ian Goetzinger. Used with permission.

FIGURE 2.4: School District of Greenfield's G21 impacts.

EdLeader21

EdLeader21 is an organization that seeks to support collaborative efforts among progressive schools and districts committed to 21st century learning goals. I began working with EdLeader21 in 2012 on what became known as STEP21, a peer review process designed to provide member schools and districts with perspective and feedback regarding their progress in achieving these goals.

Early in the design process for STEP21, it became apparent that we didn't want schools to simply list the things they were doing to promote 21st century learning. We wanted to help them focus on the results of these efforts. What tangible evidence might they collect in order to assess their progress toward these goals? We used the I-O-I framework within this peer review process to help distinguish between organizations' efforts (inputs and outputs) and real evidence that their students were achieving the desired learning goals (impacts). The intent was to help schools and districts focus on the achievement of their impacts. To do so, we asked them to provide evidence of inputs, outputs, and impacts separately for review and feedback. Reinforcing the difference between organizational actions and products and evidence of student learning directly related to 21st century learning goals was one of our aims. This proved challenging for the learning organizations involved, as schools tend to have lots of evidence of inputs and outputs and not so much for impacts, but it also led a number of them to shift their focus toward the premise behind I-O-I.

Beijing City International School

Beijing City International School is a midsize English-language international school in Beijing, China. In 2015, it had a progressive vision to create new and powerful learning opportunities for its students alongside its well-established International Baccalaureate (IB) programs, but it was in need of a protocol to provide focus and direction. In response to this commitment, they initiated the design of the IDEATE program. However, the school was somewhat distracted by a number of hows and lacked clarity around the why and what of its goals.

When I began working with the school, we started with a small design team to really understand the difference between ends and means. We worked hard to establish a set of core impacts that the teachers, program leaders, and administration believed were essential for their students. From there, we articulated a set of concrete indicators for those impacts and ways in which we would support providing concrete feedback to students and guide them to self-assess in these areas. Then we could get to the how through two challenging questions: (1) What implications will our commitment to collecting and interpreting evidence of impacts have for how we do things (assessment design, grading, reporting, and so on)? and (2) What instructional and learning approaches will best help students gain, develop, practice, and demonstrate these impacts at high levels? This resulted in a practical model and framework for the development of a cohesive, meaningful, and transformative learning program as demonstrated in figure 2.5 (page 32).

Source: © 2018 by Beijing City International School. Used with permission.

FIGURE 2.5: Program model for Beijing City International School's IDEATE program.

We worked to identify the program's goals as impacts, which we further unpacked as performance areas (which we will discuss in chapter 3, page 47). Key pathways to learning were also identified to support the development and demonstration of the impacts. These were experiential learning, transfer of learning, self-directed learning, and social-emotional learning. The school's IDEATE coordinator, Megan Eddington, explains:

> Working with the I-O-I framework helped our team focus on what was important to us as a learning community. This gave a strong foundation in building a framework for our new high school program, IDEATE, based on our mission, vision, and philosophy. The impacts developed formed the basis of our curriculum, unit planning, and feedback and assessment. It has given us confidence to transform our thinking and practice of teaching and learning in the secondary school, knowing that we are focused on student outcomes. (M. Eddington, personal communication, September 8, 2018)

New England Association of Schools and Colleges' Commission on International Education

The New England Association of Schools and Colleges (NEASC) provides accreditation services for public, private, collegiate, and international educational organizations. It has been doing so successfully since 1885. But in 2014, the then-head of the NEASC Commission on International Education, Peter Mott, became convinced that there had to be a better way than the document-heavy, compliance-focused accreditation protocols and processes of the past. His goal was not just to put applicants through a mechanical quality check and give them a stamp of approval, but to encourage schools to move from improvement to transformation with a focus on learning. Out of this premise, the ACE (architecture, culture, and ecology) accreditation protocol was born.

As part of a small initial design team for ACE, I introduced I-O-I and, particularly, the notion of impacts as a learning-focused articulation of an organization's mission. It was just one piece of the overall framework, but it did help provide the learning focus missing from past accreditation protocols.

ACE flips the script on the usual accreditation process and focus. Instead of targeting the organization's action and documentation (the inputs and outputs), it hones in on evidence that a learning community is achieving its learning principles through impacts. Prior accreditation processes often chose to assume that the right documentation and organization structures generated desired learning. Mott explains this difference:

> The I-O-I concept replaces schools'—and previous accreditation protocols'—fondness for focusing on outputs (e.g., programs, activities, and events) with the expectation that evidence of observable and demonstrable learning impacts be provided. In doing so, the Input-Output-Impact model promotes design thinking, challenges cherished assumptions about schooling, and implicitly proposes a new paradigm for K–12 education—a fundamental objective of ACE. (P. Mott, personal communication, August 18, 2018)

ACE looks at learning first and then looks at the level to which the organization is, or isn't, supporting the desired, mission-driven learning through intentional and purposeful design and action.

Conclusion

Educators and educational systems need to reframe their thinking and pursue the transformational learning goals that students truly need and deserve. Past change efforts and the enormous amounts of resources they have expended have not proved very successful. I-O-I provides not only a way for us to shift our thinking and approach to change but also a framework to guide our efforts. In and of itself, it's not radical. It's not the I-O-I framework itself but its implications that create this transformational potential.

In the next chapter, we will explore a number of methodologies, strategies, and processes for creating clear, future-focused goals and operationalizing impacts.

Chapter 2 Resources

School and district teams can use the following questions and activities to put the concepts from this chapter into action. Teams should retain artifacts resulting from these exercises to inform later work.

Collaborative Inquiry

Consider the following questions, then discuss your answers as a team.

- What are the long-term impact goals for our strategic work?
- How do we report the progress and success of our strategic work to our community and governing body?
- How do we know if our inputs and outputs have been successful?
- How might the achievement of inputs and outputs differ from the achievement of impacts?

Collaborative Activities

The following activities will help you and your team operationalize the ideas from this chapter. Each activity builds on the one before it, so we recommend completing them in the order shown. Be sure to review the instructions in advance and gather any needed materials, such as markers and chart paper.

Goal Check

As a team, do a brief scan of your current strategic plan. How many of the goals therein are impacts, and how many are outputs? What do they actually measure or report on? Take a similar approach with an annual progress report, if your organization has one. What do these documents tell you?

Connect the Dots

Often, schools and districts can construct simple mission statements from the impacts they've identified, deriving a concise statement from the core transformational goals for learning directly. However, I often work with schools and districts that are not engaged in developing new mission statements, but wish to do something concrete with the mission they have. In this case, we can simply extract clear goals from existing statements, as opposed to going back through the whole process of developing new statements. As a follow-up to the Word Salad activity in chapter 1 (page 18), display a printed copy of your department's, school's, or district's mission and vision statements. Identify a small number of core transformational learning goals (impacts) your team has previously discussed, and write these between your existing statements. Use the following prompts to explore connections.

- Can we draw connecting lines between part of the statements and one or more of our impacts?
- How do our impacts help answer the mission-focused question, What does that look like?
- Can we describe our mission or vision through our impacts?
- After we have connected elements of our statements to our impacts, what is left that does not align? Is it useful?

Looking for Evidence

The previous chapter focused on identifying what learning goals lie at the heart of your mission and vision. You also looked for evidence of those goals. Moving a little deeper on this front, select an impact, and discuss what evidence of student learning you might collect to see if students are developing toward that impact. For example, the impact goal of global citizenship might require collecting student evidence related to cultural awareness, global issues, empathy, or systems thinking. Simply brainstorm a list of artifacts or evidence that might appropriately demonstrate these things.

Planning Template for the Input-Output-Impact Framework

Please note that an output should be accompanied by a number of inputs.

Impact:					
Outputs	Inputs	Time Frame for Completion	Who Is Responsible	Resources Needed	Actions Needed

CHAPTER 3

HOW

Putting Impacts at the Center

Up to this point, we have learned that there is something fundamentally wrong with how we have pursued educational change, which has led to a lot of wasted energy and very little substantive progress to show for it. We also discussed I-O-I as a framework that can guide thinking and actions in much more effective and lasting ways. This chapter will address the first in a series of hows—strategies and processes for enacting the framework. The driving question for this chapter is simple: How might we choose and act on essential learning impacts for our students?

Most of this chapter focuses on teaching and learning structures, such as assessment and curriculum design. Specifically, the upcoming sections encourage educators to do three things: (1) focus on the future, (2) clarify goals, and (3) operationalize impacts. Since I-O-I is learning centered, learning goals drive planning and organizational goal setting.

Educators need clarity about essential goals for student learning. It is not enough to have a few broad, ambiguous words, such as *collaboration* and *critical thinking*. If we leave planning and goal setting at that level and do not dig into our students' future needs, we risk ending up where we have often ended up: with broad aspirations but no real way to address or assess them with purpose or validity.

Focus on the Future

Importantly, I-O-I is derived from a student-centered approach, not an organization-centered one. All work must center on student learning needs and goals. It must not just prepare students for the next year's standards or college entrance, but meet the much larger responsibility to help them learn for life, whatever that life may look like in the ambiguous future.

Many educational thought leaders discuss the need to change not only how we teach but what we teach. In short, they say we must look to the best research and thought on how the future might unfold so we can articulate what students really need to learn. For example, Heidi Hayes Jacobs and Marie Hubley Alcock (2017) write about the need to contemporize the hows and whats of learning in their book *Bold Moves for Schools: How We Create Remarkable Learning Environments*. Jacobs and Alcock advocate for examining what (as well as how) we currently teach as either antiquated (and may need to go), classical (still important), or contemporary (new learning goals for new realities). This process can be useful in clearing out what is no longer useful and targeting what is now essential.

To be clear, this does not mean throwing away traditional learning goals (the classical). However, we must reposition these traditional goals (academic standards) as the starting point for modern learning, not the end goal. As David N. Perkins (2014) succinctly puts it, we must move beyond what we currently do and address his six "beyonds":

1. Beyond content—21st century skills, competencies, etc., such as critical and creative thinking, collaboration, communication, self-management
2. Beyond local—Global perspectives, problems, and studies, as with our global economy or worldwide problems of energy or water supplies
3. Beyond topics—Content as tools for thinking and action, for instance with regard to some of the big issues above
4. Beyond the traditional disciplines—Renewed and extended visions of the disciplines, for instance broader views of history or studies of contemporary communication technologies
5. Beyond discrete disciplines—Interdisciplinary topics and problems, such as the roots of intergroup human conflict or poverty
6. Beyond prescribed content—Learners as choosers of what they learn well beyond the typical use of "electives" (Perkins & Chua, 2012, p. 1)

I-O-I initially focuses on the first point, moving beyond content. The implications of moving beyond content help to set the stage for the five other elements as part of a transformed learning environment. If we need to move beyond content, what do we move toward? In order to answer that question, we need to start with an informed view of the future. While we cannot predict the future, we can seek to understand what might drive the emerging future and what this might mean for our students. Building a knowledge base of the future seems like an obvious first step in seeking to understand what it means for learning. But educators often miss this first step, instead building ideas about what students will need in their futures on assumptions and misunderstandings. We need to build our impacts on understandings and insights. A list of resources you can consult to help develop an informed view of the future is available at **go.SolutionTree.com/leadership**.

For example, collaboration and critical thinking certainly existed before the dawn of the 21st century. In essence, those terms still mean much the same thing as they have forever. But the context, processes, and tools for thinking critically in a world of readily accessible (and readily manipulated) information and the ways we collaborate in a digital, globalized world are very different than those of the past. We need to develop a future focus in order to understand those variables and what they mean for functioning in the society of the future.

We must stop:

- Assuming that there is a fixed set of content knowledge that all students need to know
- Confusing information that students can easily look up with something that is worthy of the time needed for retention and recall
- Focusing our efforts on learning what *we* already know as opposed to equipping *students* for what they will need to know and the new learning they will need to create for themselves
- Basing learning-focused dialogue and decision making on what we know today
- Diminishing essential skills for learning and life in the 21st century by calling them "soft skills"

School community members should engage with relevant information (from reliable sources and targeting important drivers of change in the future) and ideas in order to identify the ways the future might shape students' lives. It is impossible to overstate the importance of engaging a smaller team in this undertaking. A large team can become unwieldy, and the process can grind to a halt. (Some resources to help start this process appear at the end of the chapter [page 51].) This process should result in a clear statement of some main insights about the emerging future. These statements about the emerging future should lead the team to ask, "What should our response be to help students prepare for this?" Then the team should arrive at the organization's targeted responses to these insights and needs, which, in effect, become the impacts. A simple table, such as table 3.1, will probably suffice to communicate the team's insights, foresight, and strategic directions that will guide the next steps. The left column distills the team's insights, grouped into logical categories. The right lists the implications of these insights and the team's conclusions. For further guidance on this process, see the second edition of *Leading Modern Learning: A Blueprint for Vision-Driven Schools* (McTighe & Curtis, 2019).

Table 3.1: Insights and Conclusions Drawn From Learning About the Future

Core Insights About the Future	Educational Conclusions
The Future Workforce	
• Our students will have many different jobs in the future, many of which do not yet exist. • Job markets and opportunities will shift rapidly with the increasing effects of robotics and outsourcing and the rising influence of artificial intelligence. • Fewer traditional full-time jobs will exist in the future. • More opportunities will develop through smaller, agile innovations than through traditional, lifelong corporate careers. • People will be living and working far beyond current norms.	• We need to prepare our students to learn continuously and to reinvent themselves throughout their lives. • Our students must be able to activate the skills and dispositions of modern learning throughout their lives. • It is no longer enough to attempt to teach our students an existing set of finite knowledge. • Schools need to shift from preparing students solely for college or lifelong careers to providing them with the skills and dispositions to navigate fluid and ambiguous work and life environments.
Knowledge and Skills	
• The workforce and some postsecondary environments highlight the need for skills and dispositions beyond those normally taught or assessed in school.	• Our students must acquire skills and dispositions beyond the traditional subject area–based content and procedural knowledge schools have traditionally delivered.

• Much of the content schools have traditionally transmitted to students that is relevant to a task or challenge is now readily available through the internet. • The future will be solution and design focused, often spanning existing disciplines or known problems.	• Retention and recall are not key skills or indicators of learning for the future. • Our students will need to demonstrate more than good grades in order to impress future employers, investors, partners, and further learning institutions. • Our students will need more experience in transferring and extending their learning through messy and complex real-world learning and tasks.
Globalization and Change	
• The world will become increasingly interdependent. • The future will become increasingly characterized by volatility, uncertainty, complexity, and ambiguity. • The tight connections between systems and people across the planet mean that things will shift more rapidly and unintended consequences will become more pronounced. • The mobility of populations will increase.	• Our students need to truly understand the interrelated nature of the world, its systems, and its people. • The fluidity with which our students can move between and among cultures will be more important. • Identifying patterns and anticipating change will be important skills for the future. • Students need to explore and understand the implications of issues, changes, and solutions within and across systems.
Technology	
• Technology and media are likely to create more polarization and disparity. • Digital crime, identity theft, and media manipulation will become more prevalent than traditional threats. • Accelerating technological advances will have far-reaching effects on relationships, communities, and life balance.	• Balance and well-being will become increasingly important for healthy and successful lives. • Students must learn to rapidly adapt to and utilize new technologies. • Students must become critical, savvy consumers and creators of information, data, and ideas.

Source: McTighe & Curtis, 2019, pp. 21–22.

Clarify Goals

With an orientation toward the future in place, a school can begin the necessary work of setting clear, transformative goals. It is not enough to identify broad ideas about modern learning; we need to clearly define and communicate what each one truly means. Without this clarity, we run the distinct risk of falling into the same sort of ambiguity that makes mission and vision statements so difficult to point to in real life. We also leave the goals open to varying interpretations, which causes confusion.

On the other hand, many organizations go down a rabbit hole, overdocumenting rather than clarifying. We don't need pages of text, but we do need simple statements that provide all stakeholders with a common understanding of our impacts. Clear yet brief definitions have the simple power of shared language and meaning. Specifically, teams should expand on the insights and implications described in the previous section (page 40) to come up with a simple understanding of each impact. Additionally, a team might devise a small number of essential questions that engage all school community members (especially students) in thinking more deeply about the impacts. Figure 3.1 displays some examples. A reproducible template appears at the end of this chapter (page 54).

Impact	Understanding	Essential Questions
Global Mindedness	An interrelated and interdependent global landscape requires that people have an engaged view of the world around us, its issues, and its complexities.	• How are people around the world linked, and how are we different? • How might perspectives on this issue vary? • What expected and unexpected consequences may arise if I take this action?
Creative Thinking	People often discover opportunities and solutions to the complexity around us from nontraditional sources, and this requires the ability to think and act in novel, innovative ways.	• What other ways might I approach this idea? • Why might this idea be of value? • What might I do with this idea?
Self-Directed Learning	Future work and life forces will require people to reinvent themselves often and seek opportunities for new learning and development throughout their lives.	• How do I learn most effectively? • How might I reach this goal? • What do I need from this learning opportunity?

FIGURE 3.1: Clarifying impacts.

These understandings and questions become an effective entry point into the organization's impacts for the entire community. All community members can engage with these to better understand the meaning of these terms, how they are important, and how students might explore them in the context of their own learning.

Operationalize Impacts

In addition to clarifying goals, we must unpack them in a format that enables their use in schools and classrooms. Well-articulated learning goals are as essential for impacts as for any traditional subject area. Could you imagine any school having a learning goal called *mathematics* without breaking it down into narrower, more specific topics and standards? Why would we treat impacts, like global mindedness, any differently? However, schools commonly leave these mission-centered learning goals in a vague state that teachers cannot address and students cannot demonstrate. As such, these goals become reporting categories at best. Teachers address them with a broad anecdotal comment on a report card, and give minimal evidence to back it up. Clearly, this will not sufficiently help students develop and demonstrate impacts to a desired level. Instead, we should provide feedback when students specifically demonstrate impacts on particular tasks for which using those skills and dispositions is essential to success.

We should unpack impacts in a manner similar to how we unpack academic subject areas, moving toward greater clarity that supports operationalizing these learning goals. Figure 3.2 shows a basic, generic structure for how we articulate traditional academic subject areas.

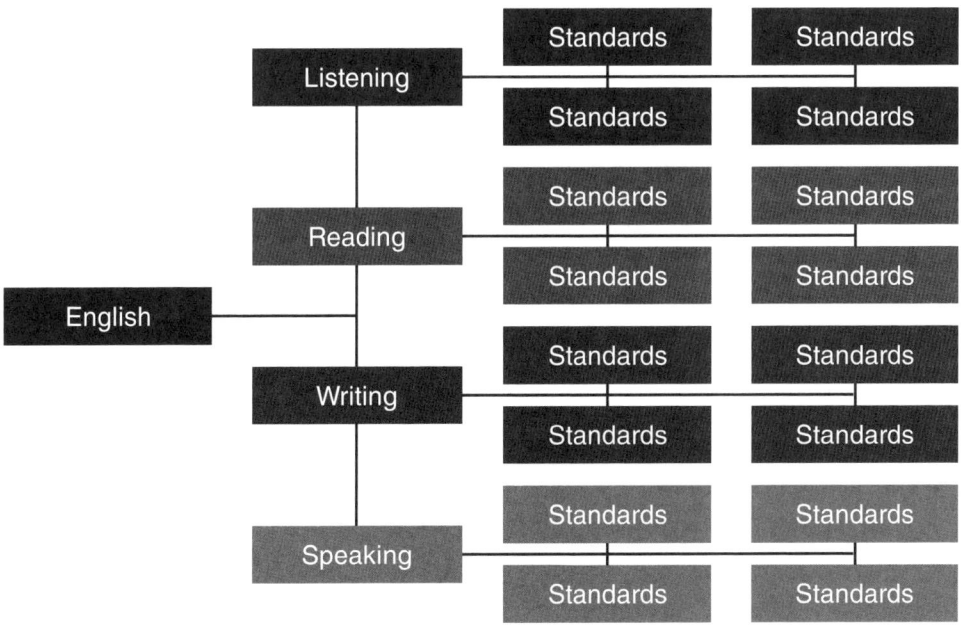

FIGURE 3.2: Subject-area unpacking structure for English language arts.

Why not do the same for impacts (see figure 3.3)? Far more useful than composing lengthy definitions is unpacking impacts into more specific performance areas and developmentally appropriate performance indicators. This process compliments the processes discussed previously (insights, implications, understandings, and questions) by providing examples of the types of things that students might do in order to demonstrate the impact.

To clarify, each term in figure 3.3 is defined as follows.

- **Impact:** Mission-centered, transformational goal for learning
- **Performance areas:** Key aspects of the impact
- **Performance indicators:** Age-appropriate, demonstrable, and assessable examples of the desired level of learning for each performance area

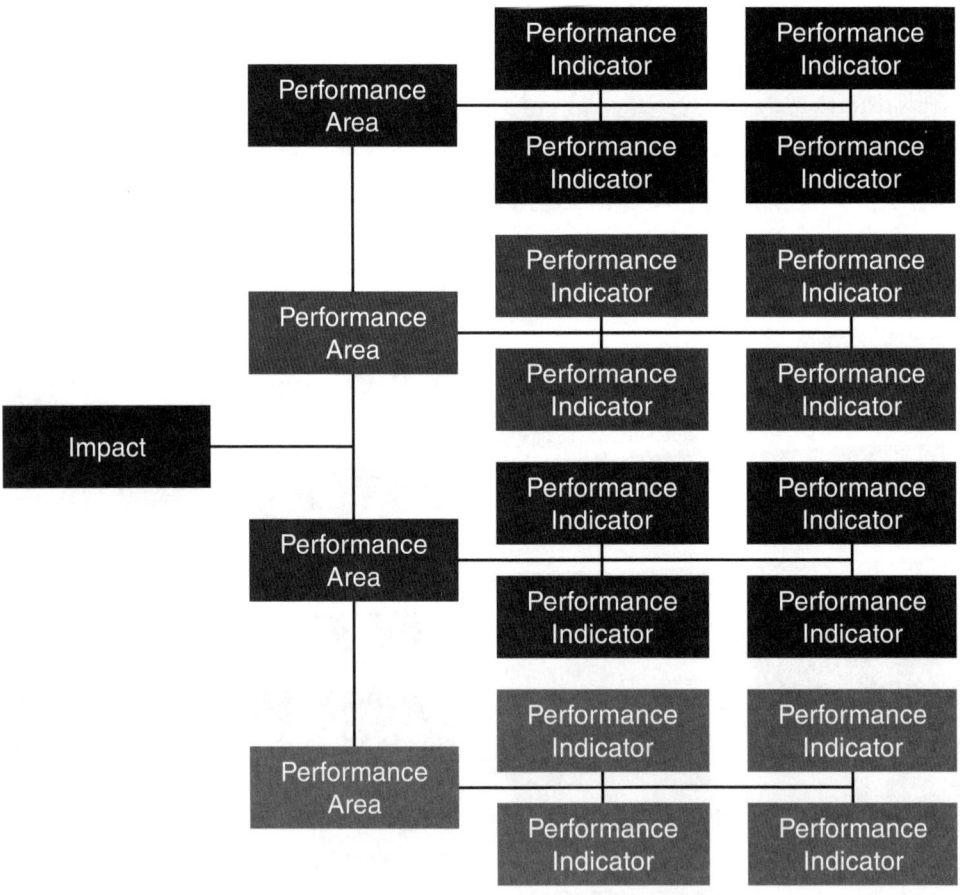

FIGURE 3.3: Impact articulation structure.

In addition, a school should have tools and strategies that students can use to enact various performance areas and demonstrate performance indicators, which we will discuss in chapter 5 (page 81). The following sections explore performance areas and performance indicators in more depth.

We must stop:

- Giving mission-centered goals the flyby treatment
- Living with broad terms and vague language
- Succumbing to the temptation to write lengthy academic definitions and documents instead of using real examples of what learning might look like through performance indicators
- Claiming that we already do something if we have no substantial evidence of student learning to prove it

Performance Areas

If a school or district has articulated its impacts, it will often leave them in broad, nebulous terms. In my experience, failing to unpack an impact into a small set of component parts will leave the impact as an inaccessible goal open to many interpretations and little focus. This is similar to the example of unpacking an English curriculum into strands, which builds a bridge between the whole topic (English) and individual standards that students can demonstrate (verifying information gathered through a research process, for example).

When it comes to impacts, we may choose to unpack a huge impact like global mindedness into performance areas such as cultural literacy, systems thinking, empathy, and global awareness (see figure 3.4).

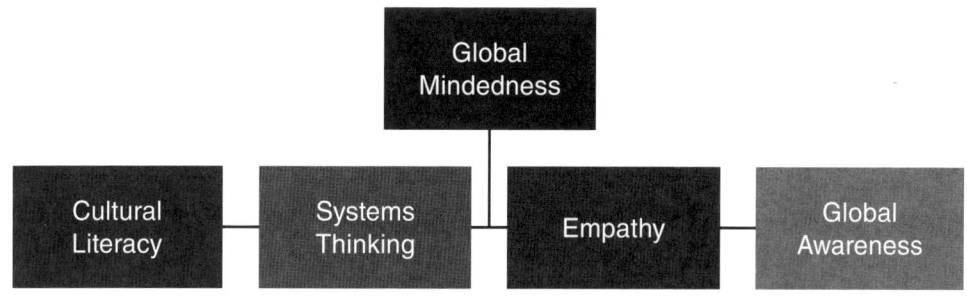

FIGURE 3.4: Sample performance areas for global mindedness.

This work can be time-consuming if a team starts from scratch. Educators might find a starter list of potential performance areas beneficial for beginning the unpacking discussion and process. They might use examples such as those in the appendix (page 125) or connect with another school that has already undertaken this process.

Note that the goal of this process is not to create an indisputable list of performance areas; rather, it aims to create a list that highlights the important, future-focused aspects of each impact that the school or district wants to focus on. The example in figure 3.4 seeks not to state *everything* about global mindedness, but rather to direct our common understanding of an expansive topic and prioritize our focus areas within it.

Performance Indicators

Performance areas bring us one step closer to fully operational impacts. But we're not quite there yet. We still need to break performance areas down into age-appropriate desired actions and demonstrations, called *performance indicators*. A performance indicator is not a standard. It is an example of the type of thing that a student at a particular developmental stage would do to demonstrate a desired level of performance or development in a performance area. They help students, parents, and teachers focus on the demonstration of desired learning through evidence.

It is advisable to unpack performance areas into performance indicators for grade bands—for example, preK–2, grades 3–5, grades 6–8, and grades 9–12. Trying to create individual grade-specific indicators would be overly complicated and unnecessarily restrictive. Figure 3.5 presents an example for global mindedness in grades 3–5. A reproducible worksheet to guide this process appears at the end of this chapter (page 55).

Performance indicators are *not* an exhaustive list of standards or criteria to check off. Instead, they are meant to briefly describe the types of things (among many) that students could do to demonstrate their skills and dispositions. They are examples of demonstrable traits and elements of these skills. They are not and never will be perfect, comprehensive, all-encompassing, or immune to criticism. In other words, they could be picked apart endlessly, but my advice is to reach relative agreement and try them out instead of endlessly wordsmithing them in isolation. In addition, teams should consider a set of performance indicators a living document and enhance the set over time.

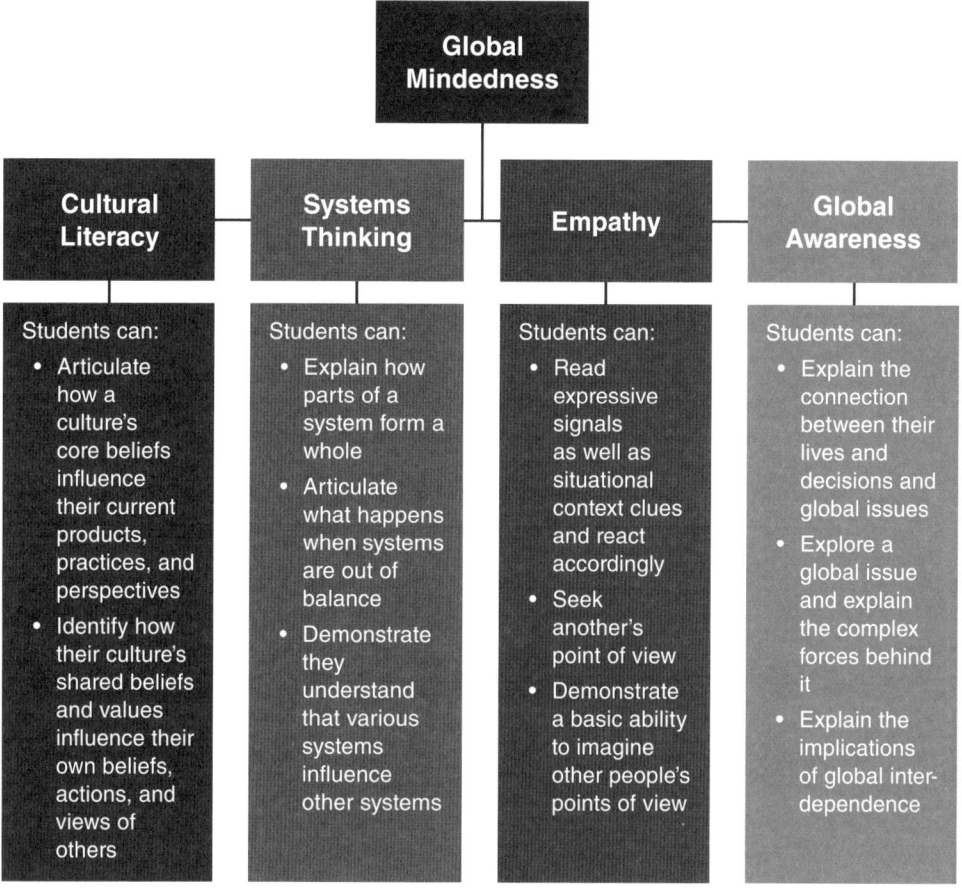

FIGURE 3.5: Sample performance areas and indicators for global mindedness, grades 3–5.

While unpacking skills and dispositions, like empathy or critical thinking, into age-appropriate indicators may be a new challenge for many, teams can find additional guidance in the great deal of research and writing on the topic. Much work has been done in the areas of social-emotional learning and positivist psychology, for example. One place to start is *Identifying Indicators and Tools for Measuring Social and Emotional Healthy Living: Children Ages 5–12 Years* (Schonert-Reichl, Lawlor, Oberle, & Thomson, 2009), which provides important background information about students' social-emotional health, as well as definitions and indicators of many social-emotional skills (additional resources for performance indicators are listed at **go.SolutionTree.com/leadership**). Just because we have not operationalized impacts before and may find it difficult does not mean that we should not do it now.

Finally, we need to get breakdowns of performance areas and indicators into teachers' and students' hands early in the process. Leaders should provide teachers with performance areas and indicators for their age level and ask them to look for demonstrations of performance indicators. They can also add some of their own that they feel provide valid evidence. Teachers should also introduce performance areas and indicators to students, discuss them with their classes, and allow students to identify examples from personal experience. Educators tend to labor over documents and programs, trying to make them perfect before they distribute them. Something like this, however, will never be perfect. Those most closely involved with enacting impacts—namely, teachers and students—need the chance to play with them, mold them, and make them their own. Often teachers will add indicators to the list or work with their students to reword indicators in student-friendly language with examples. Displaying performance areas and indicators around the room and posting evidence and examples with them are also techniques that engender positive results. We want to provide educators with resources and guidance, not make them feel like we have handed them a rigid and immovable recipe.

Conclusion

The process of defining and operationalizing impacts should result in a comprehensive set of performance areas and performance indicators. These elements guide the curriculum we design to help students gain the skills and dispositions within impacts. They also communicate the ways in which students can demonstrate these skills at an appropriate level. In the next chapter, we will move to another element of how, namely, assessing for impacts.

Chapter 3 Resources

School and district teams can use the following questions and activities to put the concepts from this chapter into action. Teams should retain artifacts resulting from these exercises to inform later work.

Collaborative Inquiry

Consider the following questions, then discuss your answers as a team.

- What does our learning about the future tell us about new challenges and opportunities our students might face?
- How might we help students address these opportunities and challenges with skill and confidence?
- What makes our impacts different now from how we may have thought about them in the past? How has the context changed?
- What performance areas are important for us to focus on, and how do we state them simply? How might we move beyond the generic and create modern performance areas?
- What might a student do to demonstrate these performance areas?
- What implications do the answers to the preceding questions have for teachers?

Collaborative Activities

The following activities will help you and your team operationalize the ideas from this chapter. Each activity builds on the one before it, so we recommend completing them in the order shown. Be sure to review the instructions in advance and gather any needed materials, such as markers and chart paper.

Pin the Tail on the Future

As part of building an informed view of the future, develop a future narrative or imagine future artifacts to help gather your team's learning in a more concrete way. This helps the team bring shared learning into focus and develop insights. Remember, however, you are exploring the possible future that awaits your students, not trying to predict it in definitive terms. Try some of the following prompts.

- Create a day-in-the-life narrative for a thirty-year-old person in 2040.
- Make a video diary entry or a daily schedule for a ninth-grade student in 2025.
- Create some advertisements for new jobs in 2030.
- Develop a sample transcript or college application for 2030.
- Write a job description for an educator in 2035.

Again, the goal here is to explore the future in creative and engaging ways. This can also help create illustrative artifacts that vividly communicate the team's learning in appealing ways.

Define Performance Areas

After you have articulated a manageable number of impacts, develop a few performance areas for each. To get going, you can use the starter list in the appendix (page 125) or ask the following questions.

- What does this impact look like in a modern context? How might it differ from past understandings?
- What do we feel is important to focus on as performance areas of this impact, and why?
- What does a person who excels at this impact do well?
- What are the chunks or segments to doing or fulfilling this impact?
- Can the performance area be demonstrated and observed?
- Is the performance area important to all subject areas and ages? Why and how?

Define Performance Indicators

Once you have arrived at the performance areas for your impacts, you will need to brainstorm some possible performance indicators to populate the grade bands. You can find some resources for sample performance indicators online at **go.SolutionTree.com/leadership**. The following eleven-step activity can begin to fill in the blanks. It is meant to be tactile and relatively quick, and lead to dialogue.

1. Gather sample indicators for your impacts or use some from this book's list or another existing resource. Print and cut these out so that each possible indicator is on its own slip of paper. These samples should span all grade levels. Categorize these indicators by impact, and write the name of each impact on the outside of its own large envelope. Put the indicators in the impact envelope they correspond to.

2. On blank poster paper, create a grid like the following.

	Impact: _____		
Grade Bands	Performance Area: _____	Performance Area: _____	Performance Area: _____
PreK–2			
3–5			
6–8			
9–12			

3. Divide your team into groups of three or four people. Give one impact envelope and grid to each group. Ask the groups to write their impact and performance areas in the appropriate boxes. Provide them with glue sticks and sticky notes.

4. Ask each group to empty its envelope of sample performance indicators.

5. Provide groups with forty-five minutes to sort their pile of indicators under the appropriate performance areas and grade bands. They can also use sticky notes to add new indicators where they see fit.

6. Encourage lots of talk, but also advise groups not to get stuck on details at this stage.

7. After the work period, do a brief gallery walk so that everyone can see how each impact is coming together.

8. Photograph each piece of poster paper. Transcribe the posters' text into a digital document, and distribute that document to groups a few days later.

9. Give groups the opportunity to tweak their work a bit. These adjustments would occur on each group's own time over the course of perhaps two weeks.

10. Distribute the resulting drafts to willing teachers at various grade levels. (Only give them the content for their grade bands, or else they may become overwhelmed.)

11. Ask these teachers to look at the performance indicator grids over the next couple of weeks and respond to some simple questions, such as:

    - Does the basic structure (impact to performance area to performance indicator) make sense to you?
    - Do you already recognize some of these performance indicators in your classroom?
    - When and how do your students demonstrate some of these?
    - Are the indicators appropriately challenging so that they represent where we want our students to get to, rather than where they are?
    - What other indicators might you add?
    - How might you help your students understand these?

The goal of this activity is to relatively quickly prototype impacts, performance areas, and performance indicators, and to engage teachers in that process. You don't want to get bogged down trying to make everything perfect. If you've worked with committees on academic standards, you know that this can take an inordinate amount of time and kill enthusiasm. You are not after a concrete checklist of impact standards. You want to engage people in trying out these indicators and developing them in a thoughtful manner. Also, you want them to understand the structure being employed.

Goal-Clarification Template

Impact	Understanding	Essential Questions

Template for Operationalizing Impacts

Impact:			
Performance Areas			
High School Indicators			
Middle School Indicators			
Upper–Elementary School Indicators			
Lower–Elementary School Indicators			
Impact:			
Performance Areas			
High School Indicators			
Middle School Indicators			
Upper–Elementary School Indicators			
Lower–Elementary School Indicators			
Impact:			
Performance Areas			
High School Indicators			
Middle School Indicators			
Upper–Elementary School Indicators			
Lower–Elementary School Indicators			

Moving Beyond Busy © 2020 Solution Tree Press • SolutionTree.com
Visit **go.SolutionTree.com/leadership** to download this free reproducible.

Impact:			
Performance Areas			
High School Indicators			
Middle School Indicators			
Upper–Elementary School Indicators			
Lower–Elementary School Indicators			
Impact:			
Performance Areas			
High School Indicators			
Middle School Indicators			
Upper–Elementary School Indicators			
Lower–Elementary School Indicators			

CHAPTER 4

HOW
Assessing for Impacts

As Carol Ann Tomlinson (2018) states, "Before we decide *how* to measure, we must decide *what* matters most" (p. 90). Having established what matters most—impacts—we can move on to the important tasks of teaching and assessing students. This chapter will focus on how we can assess student performance and growth at a task-based level. Impacts are the desired results; teachers must collect acceptable evidence of student learning (Wiggins & McTighe, 2005). In short, we will address the fundamental question, How will we know that our intended learning is actually happening? To answer this question, we'll discuss how to articulate different types of learning, shift our thinking about assessment, make impacts assessable, and simplify feedback practices.

Articulating Different Types of Learning

Impacts require a different approach to assessment. They are not binary, so we cannot assess them in the same way we might measure the number of right or wrong answers on a math test. Instead of measuring, we need to qualitatively interpret evidence as to the level to which the student has demonstrated the desired impact within a specific task. But, we also need to associate some data with our qualitative feedback or we will not be able to adequately look for growth over time. In order to provide valuable, actionable feedback to learners, we need a way to quantify qualitative feedback. This may seem contradictory, but the feedback we give must consistently and coherently describe the level to which a student is demonstrating a performance area. We cannot just say, "Good job," and expect students to do much with that feedback, nor can we extract any useful data from such feedback. We must find a way to quantify the qualitative.

We first need to recognize the type of learning that a performance area represents and ensure that the mode of feedback aligns with that learning type. Often, we lump different types of transdisciplinary learning together, leaving no effective way to provide appropriate feedback. We need to articulate lists of aspirational learning goals that contain different types of learning and reinforce them through appropriate metrics. Learning goals vary in nature. Critical thinking is not the same type of learning goal as, say, growth mindset or resilience.

There are three types of transdisciplinary learning that schools frequently lump together: (1) values, (2) cognitive skills, and (3) dispositions. Let's define the categories.

- **Values:** Principles, morals, and beliefs held by individuals and groups that guide actions and interactions
- **Cognitive skills:** Skills that transcend subject areas and help students successfully learn by using tools and strategies to create and work with information and processes
- **Dispositions:** Qualities, tendencies, and characteristics that form a habitual way of acting and reacting

Table 4.1 lists examples of these categories.

Table 4.1: Different Types of Transdisciplinary Learning

Values	Cognitive Skills	Dispositions
• Integrity	• Critical thinking	• Resilience
• Kindness	• Creative thinking	• Adaptability
• Ethics	• Inquiry	• Empathy
• Tolerance	• Collaboration	• Growth mindset

Of course, one could argue that these types of learning have crossover. For instance, can you be a good creative thinker without adaptability? Can you collaborate without empathy? Certainly, these elements engage with one another, and we should not artificially isolate them. The goal is to tailor the approach to these types of learning to their unique characteristics. Schools might write their own definitions; regardless, students neither acquire, develop, nor demonstrate them in the same ways, and therefore, educators should not assess different types of learning in the same way.

Values are essential for schools, as they represent shared agreements about how the school community will learn together. Teachers and administrators can highlight them, model them, and celebrate when students demonstrate them, but it is not appropriate to treat them the same way as we treat cognitive skills or dispositions. We cannot live together without shared values, but we cannot provide feedback on the level to which a student demonstrated integrity, for example. How would a teacher design an assessment task where integrity or kindness is a required criterion? Again, every organization and community must discuss, identify, and live by its core values. However, I do not believe that we should treat them as learning goals to be assessed.

On the other hand, we can certainly design learning experiences and assessments around cognitive skills. Many sets of content-area standards contain broad cognitive skills. Teachers can provide direct instruction on various cognitive skills, devise ways for students to practice their use, and then assess how well students use them. They can introduce a tool or strategy and ask students to use it in a particular task. For example, a teacher might introduce mind mapping (a tool to support critical thinking), have students map the various elements of an issue, and then assess the level to which each student used the strategy to complete the task successfully.

Dispositions are also teachable and learnable. For example, students can develop resilience or a growth mindset through instruction and practice. Teachers can provide feedback on how well a student activated a disposition while working on a task, but dispositions require a different, less straightforward approach than we might use with cognitive skills. For dispositions, we become less didactic and curriculum focused (in the traditional sense) and assume the role of experience designer. For example, a teacher might give students more latitude in carrying out a complex task so that the experience will activate more levels of adaptability and resilience than a teacher-driven task. The teacher could ask students to keep a project diary and identify points when they need to use tools and strategies of resilience or adaptability in order to overcome a challenge. Similarly, we might develop goal-setting experiences for students where the growth mindset is central to the process and its products. We can design project-based learning experiences where the teacher introduces wild cards at various points that require students to use a certain disposition to deal with the complication (for example, a wild card might say, "An environmental group is protesting your proposed building project; use empathy to find a solution"). It is essential that educators create opportunities for dispositions to come to the fore in a purposeful way.

Figure 4.1 illustrates how performance areas and performance indicators might look for different types of learning goals. Within the impact of global mindedness, we may have performance areas that are cognitive or dispositional in nature. Note the differences in the types of performance indicators. For cognitive skills, tools and their proficient use are more prominent. For dispositions, experience design and student action rise to the fore.

Impact	Global Mindedness	
Performance Area	Systems thinking	Empathy
Type of Learning Goal	Cognitive skill	Disposition
Performance Indicators	• Demonstrates how complex systems affect everyday life around the world • Explains how specific actions affect what happens in the short term and the long term • Demonstrates how cause and effect occur in a circular fashion • Describes change as a series of events that are connected in time to produce a particular pattern of behavior • Creates a representation or model to represent the interactions between two or more systems	• Seeks another's point of view • Demonstrates an ability to articulate other people's points of view • Demonstrates a greater understanding and appreciation of the different strengths of diverse people • Approaches problem solving with various perspectives in mind • Can adapt to deal effectively with contrasting perspectives

FIGURE 4.1: Operationalizing different types of learning goals.

On the whole, we must acknowledge the different types of learning embodied in impacts and treat them according to their unique characteristics. Most performance areas are either cognitive skills or dispositions, both of which students can learn and demonstrate. Teachers can interpret demonstrations and provide effective assessment feedback on each type. Now we will take on the difficult question, How do we assess these goals?

Shifting Our Thinking About Assessment

Tomlinson (2018) offers a thought about shifting the ways in which we assess learning:

> Right now, what we measure, over and over and over—with little regard to the damage the measuring (and the long process leading up to the measuring) may do to young people and their teachers—is the capacity to attend to, store, retrieve, and repeat bits of information and skills too often devoid of meaning. (p. 90)

If our goals have moved beyond retention, beyond recall, and beyond content (Perkins, 2014), then so, too, should our views about assessment and how we assess.

Certainly, it would be challenging to enact impacts as essential learning goals without adjusting approaches to assessment. Often teachers challenge this idea of adjusting assessment, stating that it is "impossible to measure" the concepts that typically make up impacts. If we think of assessment only as quantitative measurement, they have a valid point. How would you give a student a B on self-directed learning, let alone a grade of 75 percent on empathy? True, we cannot precisely measure impacts in this way. But, if we broaden our idea of assessment beyond binary (right-or-wrong) measurement tools and generic grades, we can take another view. In some cases, assessment is measuring, but it can also be as simple (and powerful) as providing feedback. Life outside school—where cognitive skills and dispositions are essential—does not provide grades and percentages, but it does provide plenty of other information that helps us understand how well we did or whether we are improving. Frequent feedback from a teacher, a peer, or oneself is the engine that drives growth and understanding about performance. However, this feedback must be qualitative and tied to specific tasks and evidence.

Qualitative Feedback

Impacts represent higher-order skills and dispositions and cannot be thought of in binary terms. We can't apply the same methodology as when, for example, student A gets three out of ten words wrong on the spelling test, or student B uses a mathematical algorithm correctly in four out of five instances. With impacts, we assess not *whether* a student demonstrates creative thinking, for example, but rather the *level to which* he or she uses idea generation strategies (the vehicle) to successfully solve a complex dilemma (the goal). As another example, we would not grade a student on whether he or she is resilient. Everyone has some amount of resilience, but teachers can provide students with feedback on how well they enacted this disposition to succeed in a challenging context. Our feedback must be qualitative in order to suit the nature of these learning goals. However, this does not mean that feedback on impacts will be purely subjective.

Qualitative research methodology hints at how teachers might apply metrics and organize feedback. Many social sciences, including much of education research, widely use qualitative research. Qualitative research is usually characterized by the interpretation of observations and evidence through an identified lens. Researchers do not deal with measurement until they have carried out the proper interpretation and methodology for the given evidence. One such qualitative research methodology is *coding*. Coding is when researchers examine qualitative evidence, such as interviews, surveys, and narratives, with a precise idea of what they are looking for. For example, researchers may identify phrases and words that indicate an interviewee's positive or negative attitude toward an issue. They then review each response from each subject, identify instances of these words and phrases, and code responses based on the words' and phrases' prevalence. This assessment produces the data to which they can then apply more quantitative analytical tools. The same applies when we provide feedback on impacts as desired learning goals. If we clearly identify what we are looking for by defining performance areas and indicators, we can provide valid feedback on what we observe in student evidence or demonstration of an impact.

Some teachers will say that this qualitative feedback method feels totally subjective and cannot be valid, but there are two important rebuttals to that position. First, many of the feedback and grading methods we currently use contain subjective elements. We constantly include grades and reporting categories for effort or engagement with very little defined evidence. Learning is complex, and we cannot and should not erase all subjectivity from the process.

Second, this feedback is not baseless. We, as professionals, use agreed-on criteria (performance indicators) as the basis for interpreting specific pieces of evidence. For example, English teachers use their professional judgment to interpret and grade students' writing, but they do so based on clear expectations (or standards) of what good writing looks like at that stage of development. And in much the same way, teachers can use performance indicators to provide feedback on the level to which a student has demonstrated a performance area in completing a task. If we operationalize impacts as described in chapter 3 (page 45), we have a basis for using informed and professional judgment to guide qualitative feedback.

Specific Feedback

Schools struggle with the notion of 21st century skills, habits of learning, or impacts partly because their feedback on these goals tends to be too global. Often these valuable goals become part of a single anecdotal comment on a report card. We run the risk of minimizing these goals when we treat them with a broad comment, rather than concrete evidence based on student learning. Educators must support students' learning in these areas by regularly giving assessment feedback and attaching it to specific tasks and demonstrations of learning.

Ideally, we should provide students with useful feedback based on concrete demonstrations and evidence of impacts on individual tasks. It is of limited use to simply say that a student demonstrated great creativity on her robotics project on a report card (especially if the project happened months previously). The value of feedback lies in the proximity of the feedback to the task and its validity within the task—it should be immediate and specific to the context. Also, good feedback should help a student to refine and improve his or her performance, which cannot occur unless the feedback is timely and specific. If we treat these goals too broadly or provide feedback in a very generic fashion, it is not tangible or useful to students.

With a mindset for specific, qualitative feedback, we can begin to address the practical aspects of assessing impacts.

We must stop:
- Thinking of assessment as binary measurement only
- Treating all learning goals as if they were the same
- Being afraid to use our professional judgement as long as our indicators of success are clear
- Providing feedback that is vague, imprecise, or disconnected from the specific context in which learning is demonstrated

Making Impacts Assessable

In order to intentionally use impacts as learning goals, we need to treat them in the same ways we treat more traditional learning goals in our curriculum, and that includes making them assessable. We would not think of adopting a science standard without first making sure students could demonstrate it and we could build that into our assessment task design. The same principle holds true for impacts. To make impacts assessable, educators first need to know what learning they are *looking for*; then, they need evidence to *look at* that demonstrates students' learning. And they need to integrate impacts with academic content. The following sections detail these points.

Looking for and Looking at Learning

Students can only demonstrate impacts and teachers can only assess them by actively putting them into practice. For example, we can't assess students' critical thinking by asking them to list the three types of classical reasoning. That may give us an idea of what they know about the topic of critical thinking, but it doesn't show that they can think critically to an adequate level when they do a real task. To properly assess impacts, we need to make them integral to students' success on a sufficiently rich and challenging assessment task or learning experience.

The steps for operationalizing impacts outlined in chapter 3 (page 45) form the basis for interpreting evidence of impacts. The performance indicators provide criteria against which to give feedback. As mentioned previously, we can't just say, "You did a good job with your creative thinking." Instead, teachers must provide more useful feedback: "The way you grouped your ideas from the brainstorming session and looked at them alongside your goals was a good example of sifting through ideas to find a probable starting point for innovation." In order for assessment to be effective, it needs to align with a set of desired outcomes, as exemplified by the performance indicators. These outcomes are sometimes called *look-fors*—the distinct skills that teachers look for students to demonstrate.

It is not enough, however, to define what teachers should look for. In order to collect tangible evidence on which to provide feedback, teachers also need a *look-at*—a task or product to examine and interpret. Clearly, we can assess an academic standard (a look-for) through a task or product (a look-at) designed for students to demonstrate that they have met the standard. Unfortunately, educators often struggle to apply this concept to cognitive skills and dispositions as impact learning goals. Figure 4.2 shows look-fors (performance indicators) and look-ats (assessment tasks and products) for the impact of self-directed learning.

Many useful tasks and products already exist and simply need to be applied to impacts. For example, we may have simply not used student reflection to gather evidence and provide assessment feedback in the ways that figure 4.2 suggests. In other cases, educators might find that they do not currently have a mechanism with which to capture the necessary evidence—they don't have a look-at for a look-for. For example, a teacher might introduce a simple goal log as a way to provide evidence of how students use feedback. As another example, a teacher may want to review and modify the goal-setting protocol he uses with students to make sure it includes sufficient opportunities to capture evidence of student learning related to the goal.

	Self-Directed Learning	
Performance Areas	Looking for . . . (Performance Indicators)	Looking at . . . (Tasks and Products)
Goal Setting	The ability to set realistic goals based on relevant learning evidence	Teacher assessment during the goal-setting protocol, and peer feedback and student self-assessment at the end
Use of Feedback	Conscious, independent application of feedback to improve	Student reflection in goal logs, and teacher feedback during goal check-ins
Metacognition	Use of appropriate metacognitive language and descriptors	Teacher assessment during the goal-setting protocol
Resilience	The ability to see obstacles and failures as necessary parts of the learning process	Student reflection and self-assessment, and sample interviews and surveys

FIGURE 4.2: Sample look-fors and look-ats for performance areas.

Perhaps the most challenging and important part of focusing on impacts is the commitment to designing for, capturing, and interpreting rich evidence of impacts through the processes and products of student learning. If we do not commit to doing this, we will again be guilty of propagating busyness—of undertaking a lot of work without much real effect.

Integrating Impacts With Academic Content

While it is essential to create dedicated criteria (performance indicators) and tasks for impacts, we cannot assess impacts in isolation. We cannot, for example, ask a student to take a test on global mindedness or self-directed learning. Impacts are important to learning when students must combine these skills and dispositions with content knowledge and skills in order to successfully achieve a task, just as people must do in the real world. Impacts help students do something more meaningful with the disciplinary aspects of their learning. The two should go hand-in-hand in meaningful demonstrations of learning.

In order to achieve this, we need to look for opportunities to integrate impacts into subject-area assessments and, indeed, to use impacts to enrich assessment design. We might compare this to the way a fruit farmer grows a new type of apple by grafting a branch of that type onto the trunk of an existing apple tree in his orchard. The branch and the trunk grow together and eventually become one. Similarly, teachers can bring two elements—(1) content area–based learning goals and (2) impact-based learning goals—together.

When creating an assessment, consider whether a performance area of the related impact is integral to students' success on the assessment task. If the answer is yes, then integrate that performance area, and formally include it alongside academic standards in the success criteria. If the answer is no, you may want to question the depth of that assessment task. One example would be a solutions-oriented task, where students need to come up with a solution to a problem or dilemma. A teacher can assess various performance areas that are essential to student success, such as critical thinking. Or, perhaps it's a group task, and performance areas within the collaboration impact would be essential and included as assessment criteria. As long as the task authentically requires that students demonstrate the performance area, the teacher can elevate impacts and provide specific feedback. However, we should avoid tangential and inauthentic connections. A quiz that checks students' ability in adding fractions, for example, is not the best opportunity to elevate elements of critical thinking as assessment criteria—there is no authentic evidence. The underlying idea here is simple: meaningful learning activates both disciplinary learning goals and impacts. One will not likely become a successful scientist on one's scientific knowledge alone, just as one cannot become a successful entrepreneur on creative thinking alone. But, we should make sure that the connection between impacts and success on a task is a real and concrete one. Don't force it.

Figures 4.3 and 4.4 (page 68) include examples of assessment tasks that feature only academic content and assessment tasks that integrate both academic content and impacts. These examples show how we can both identify opportunities to make impacts explicit in a task alongside academic standards and use impacts as prompts to help enrich tasks. First, it's usually easiest to pick the low-hanging fruit and see what existing opportunities we simply haven't taken advantage of yet, as figure 4.3 shows. In the upper portion is a more traditional assessment task, which is solid and addresses the academic standards. The lower portion of the figure illustrates a potential upgrade on the assessment task that elevates and integrates specific performance areas and indicators with the criteria for the task. This grade 4 mathematics example does not change the nature of the task very much, but it does formally integrate relevant

How: Assessing for Impacts

performance areas of critical thinking (the impact), providing a richer assessment and feedback opportunity. The integrated task elevates the level of critical thinking required by focusing on interpretation and extrapolation rather than a simple reading of the data presented. The academic standards are met and, in effect, exceeded by the focus on higher-level critical thinking skills. Also, note that the examples are not only applicable to mathematics, but to all subject areas and can be reinforced with tools and strategies appropriate to different contexts and disciplines.

Content-Only Assessment	
Task	**Academic Criteria**
Look at the table of simple data showing the mass of a baby from one month to six months of age. Graph these data and answer the questions about dependent and independent variables, the x-axis and y-axis. The baby became sick in a certain month; see whether you can tell at what age the baby got sick and whether your graph indicates that the baby has recovered.	• **5.G.A.1:** "Use a pair of perpendicular number lines, called axes, to define a coordinate system, with the intersection of the lines (the origin) arranged to coincide with the 0 on each line and a given point in the plane." • **5.G.A.2:** "Represent real world and mathematical problems by graphing points in the first quadrant of the coordinate plane, and interpret coordinate values of points in the context of the situation."

Integrated Assessment		
Task	**Academic Criteria**	**Impact Criteria**
Look at the table of simple data showing the mass of a baby from one month to six months of age. Graph these data and answer the questions about dependent and independent variables, the x-axis and y-axis. The baby became sick in a certain month; see whether you can tell at what age the baby got sick and whether your graph indicates that the baby has recovered. How do you know?	• **5.G.A.1:** "Use a pair of perpendicular number lines, called axes, to define a coordinate system, with the intersection of the lines (the origin) arranged to coincide with the 0 on each line and a given point in the plane." • **5.G.A.2:** "Represent real world and mathematical problems by graphing points in the first quadrant of the coordinate plane, and interpret coordinate values of points in the context of the situation."	**Critical Thinking** • **Solution generation:** Students can solve a problem by collecting some important facts. • **Conclusion generation:** Students can develop explanations or draw conclusions and use the knowledge and evidence obtained to support that explanation or conclusion.

Source for standards: National Governors Association Center for Best Practices (NGA) & Council of Chief State School Officers (CCSSO), 2010b.

FIGURE 4.3: Sample integrated assessment task for grade 4 mathematics.

Next, we can challenge ourselves to enrich content-only assessment tasks by integrating impacts where they were not previously involved. Impacts and their performance areas give us an opportunity to engage students more deeply in content and allow them to demonstrate their insights. In figure 4.4, a fairly traditional assessment task for grade 5 English language arts appears in the upper portion. In the lower portion, the teacher has modified the assessment task—it still addresses the same academic content, but it also integrates performance indicators for several impact goals.

Content-Only Assessment	
Task	**Academic Criteria**
Write a plot summary of a piece of writing. Include a timeline of events. Use direct references to the text to describe an important event.	• RI.5.1: "Quote accurately from a text when explaining what the text says explicitly and when drawing inferences from the text." • RL.5.5: "Explain how a series of chapters, scenes, or stanzas fits together to provide the overall structure of a particular story, drama, or poem."

Integrated Assessment		
Task	**Academic Criteria**	**Impact Criteria**
Think of your story as communicating a journey. Create a visual map of this journey, including a legend that helps describe different parts of that journey (an obstacle, a turn, a meeting). Choose what you feel is an important point on your map, and describe, in character, what might have happened if the character chose his or her actions differently.	• RI.5.1: "Quote accurately from a text when explaining what the text says explicitly and when drawing inferences from the text." • RL.5.5: "Explain how a series of chapters, scenes, or stanzas fits together to provide the overall structure of a particular story, drama, or poem."	**Creative Thinking** • **Idea generation:** Students can use divergent thinking to expand on known ideas to create new and imaginative combinations. **Communication** • **Expressiveness:** Students can apply creative capacities to the communications they undertake. **Global Mindedness** • **Systems thinking:** Students can create a representation of a system to demonstrate its composition and behaviors. • **Empathy:** Students can imagine other people's points of view and experiences.

Source for standards: NGA & CCSSO, 2010a.

FIGURE 4.4: Sample enriched assessment task for grade 5 English language arts.

When it comes to integrating impacts with academic content, you might envision the criteria as a Venn diagram (see figure 4.5). The criteria will include academic standards, of course. Alongside the standards, we may bring in performance areas, which may be cognitive skills or dispositions. The goal is for assessment tasks to fall into the overlapping areas that represent the intersection of two or three areas.

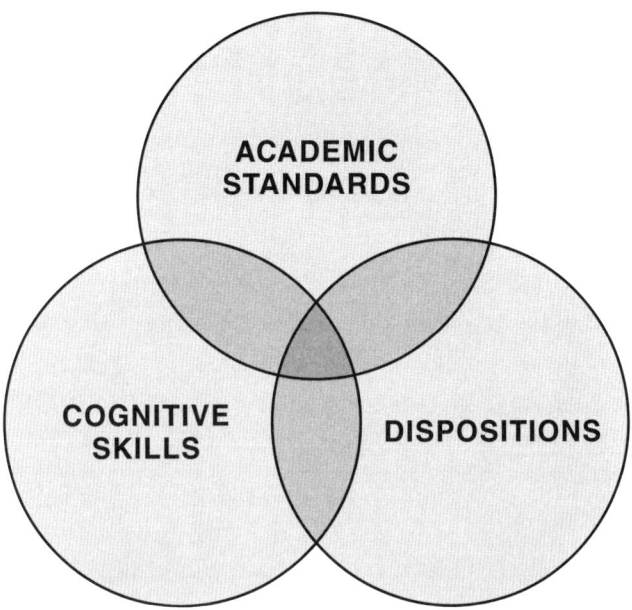

FIGURE 4.5: Integrated assessment visual.

A benefit of this focus on impacts as additional goals for learning, as I mention elsewhere, is that it tends to drive change to other elements of the learning environment. In this case, the commitment to integrating impacts as concrete and assessable elements in assessments prompts us to upgrade and modernize our assessments in order to do so. We cannot rely on antiquated assessments if we really wish to elevate impacts and collect tangible evidence of student performance and growth through our intentional designs. It is not very difficult and can really become a lever to improve assessment design because we change our goals and what evidence we want to capture and interpret via our designs.

Simplifying Feedback Practices

Many schools have struggled with truly building impacts into their curriculum for a number of reasons. First, they have not clearly articulated performance areas or performance indicators (see chapter 3, page 45). Second, schools sometimes fail to integrate impacts into assessments (see the previous sections of this chapter). Third, they often overcomplicate feedback through an overabundance of rubrics. A single grade level might use three different rubrics for creative thinking. One grade level may have its way of providing feedback on critical thinking while the next grade has a different one. A few teachers might mistakenly develop rubrics for specific tasks rather than the intended performance area and impact. All of this overcomplicates assessment and feedback and prevents students from making sense of large, long-term, transdisciplinary goals like impacts. It is also another example where the lack of an intentional framework leads to a lot of busyness that does not support the achievement of our goals. To effectively provide feedback on impacts, we must move toward simplicity.

The integration of academic content and impacts—both cognitive skills and dispositions—provides the opportunity to simplify the ways we provide feedback using common metrics. We should use these metrics across all grade levels and subject areas. They should apply to any subject area, and be designed for use with academic content, cognitive skills, and dispositions. In the following sections, we explore academic feedback, performance area feedback, and their combination.

We must stop:

- Asking students and parents to wade through a mass of confusing rubrics
- Overcomplicating assessment and grading by overusing task-specific criteria that do not connect with common learning goals
- Providing a single grade for rich learning without offering more specific feedback on students' accomplishment of different elements of the task

Academic Feedback

The standards-based assessment movement offers many methods for providing consistent feedback on students' performance as they move toward mastery or competence on a standard. Simple is often better. Consider the sliding scale of rubric levels in figure 4.6, which you can easily use on paper or in a digital learning management platform.

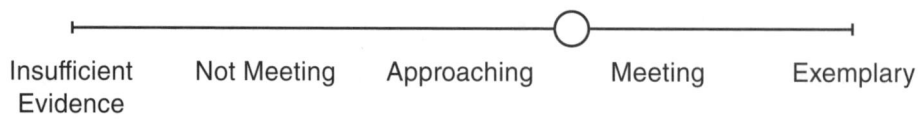

FIGURE 4.6: Standards-based grading scale.

Schools have a variety of scales they can choose from, but the move toward standards-based grading offers a versatile approach to providing feedback on both academic standards and performance areas of impacts. Figure 4.6 presents a small sample of some of the performance labels that are commonly used, but there are many others available.

Performance Area Feedback

Because assessment and feedback on impacts are new challenges for many educators, it is worth framing the discussion of performance area feedback with four main questions.

1. How can we provide valuable feedback to students on their ability to demonstrate performance areas alongside academic standards on a task-specific basis?

2. What feedback structure and system would allow students to connect and make sense of their learning across disciplines and over time?

3. How might we adequately reflect the different goals of the two types of performance areas, cognitive skills and dispositions?

4. How might we aggregate these assessment data in useful ways at both the individual and whole-school levels?

In the case of cognitive skills, answering these questions is relatively easy. Cognitive skills are more concrete than dispositions, and students must simply demonstrate proficiency in the use of related tools and strategies to be successful at a task (see chapter 5, page 82). This is pretty straightforward. Again, many proficiency-based scales are available; figure 4.7 (page 72) displays one option.

This scale is very similar to a single-point rubric. The level labeled *meeting target* represents proficiency—successful demonstration of the performance indicators for that performance area and grade band, as defined in operationalizing impacts (see chapter 3, page 45). While performance indicators provide the more specific look-fors, this scale can stay constant across all cognitive skill performance areas for all grades and subject areas. For example, we can apply this scale to provide feedback on elements of creative thinking across all disciplines and courses as the descriptors are discipline neutral. It can be used across all grades, as well. The tools and strategies may vary with the subject and level, but the descriptions as to what demonstrates different levels of proficiency are constant. This allows students to connect and interpret their demonstrations of learning both horizontally (across subjects and courses) and vertically (across years).

Not Evident	Developing	Approaching	Meeting Target	Extending
Elements of this skill have not been demonstrated. **Note:** This is not a 0 but a null—the teacher has no evidence of the student's skill level. This score is not included in the consolidation of performance data.	When prompted, the student applies this skill by following the provided or sample tools and strategies.	The student consciously and independently applies tools and strategies appropriate to an assigned task.	The student applies tools and strategies in novel situations.	The student extends and adapts tools and strategies when opportunity arises.
	The student demonstrates a beginning level of performance on the indicators in the target area.	The student demonstrates an effective level of performance on some indicators in the target area.	The student demonstrates a strong level of performance on many indicators in the target area.	The student demonstrates a level of performance beyond what is expected and is very successful at the task.

FIGURE 4.7: General scale and descriptors for cognitive skills feedback.

This commonality is important in gathering data that students, parents, teachers, and the organization will find useful. It enables everyone to compare feedback across various contexts, even beyond the traditional classroom to areas such as sports, internships, clubs, service-learning opportunities, and so on.

Similar thinking applies to the challenge of providing feedback on dispositions. Unlike with cognitive skills, however, the goal is not proficiency. We cannot assess how proficient someone is at resilience or empathy. The goal is for students to develop dispositions from a relatively naïve or latent state toward a level of automaticity where they can call on these dispositions without thought or effort as the situation requires. This is a developmental goal and, as such, we need a developmental scale for providing feedback.

As an employee of Gordon Training International in the 1970s, Noel Burch developed the "Four Stages of Learning Any New Skill" (Exceptional Leaders Lab, 2017). The four stages outlined in this model are (1) unconsciously unskilled, (2) consciously unskilled, (3) consciously skilled, and (4) unconsciously skilled. The trajectory in Burch's model, a move from unknowing to automaticity, reflects our developmental goal for dispositions. Burch's stages form the inspiration for the dispositions scale (figure 4.8, page 74).

Similar to *meeting target* in the cognitive skills scale, the scale level *developed* means that the student has successfully demonstrated the performance indicators articulated for that disposition. Again, this consistent scale is useful for all dispositions. With some interaction, students, parents, and teachers easily understand these scales, and the scales can help focus qualitative feedback and provide a quantitative metric that allows for the accumulation of data on both a micro and macro scale. Using these similar scales for performance areas and academic content enables educators to integrate feedback just as they integrate these learning goals in assessment tasks.

A Combined Example

Throughout this chapter, we have established that a rich assessment task should comprise both academic standards–based goals and impacts-based goals (cognitive skills or dispositions). Figure 4.9 (page 75) displays an example of how feedback to a student on figure 4.4's (page 68) integrated assessment task might look. A reproducible template appears at the end of this chapter (page 79).

This structure, accompanied by an anecdotal comment that provides holistic feedback on overall demonstrations of learning, can provide rich feedback on learning. Rather than providing a single overall assessment grade, these scales convey rich and

Not Evident	Emerging *Unconsciously Undeveloped*	Developing *Consciously Underdeveloped*	Developed *Consciously Developed*	Highly Developed *Unconsciously Developed*
Elements of this disposition have not been demonstrated in the context of this task. **Note:** This is not a 0 but a null—the teacher has no evidence of the disposition. This score is not included in the consolidation of performance data.	The student demonstrates a capacity for this disposition as part of his or her existing set of traits.	The student can see the supporting role of this disposition in specific contexts, but cannot yet consciously apply it to the task.	The student demonstrates this disposition as part of his or her conscious efforts to be successful at this task.	The student demonstrates this disposition at a highly developed and relatively automatic level.
	This disposition is somewhat innate and undeveloped, and the student requires direct support.	This disposition is understood, but the student is yet to consciously apply tools and strategies.	The student applies tools and strategies for positive effect at a conscious level.	This disposition is firmly embedded as a positive personal trait, and the student relatively automatically transfers the disposition.
	The student demonstrates some elements of this disposition, but often with limited capability and without a great deal of conscious purpose.	The student can identify the need for this disposition, but is learning to consciously and effectively apply approaches to act in this area and succeed at the task.	The student may need limited support or direction to consciously engage this disposition.	The student enacts this disposition as part of seeking success, often automatically and effortlessly.

FIGURE 4.8: General scale and descriptors for dispositions feedback.

Academic Goals				
RI.5.1: "Quote accurately from a text when explaining what the text says explicitly and when drawing inferences from the text."	Insufficient Evidence	Not Meeting	Approaching	○ Meeting	Exemplary
RL.5.5: "Explain how a series of chapters, scenes, or stanzas fits together to provide the overall structure of a particular story, drama, or poem."	Insufficient Evidence	○ Not Meeting	Approaching	Meeting	Exemplary

Impact Goals				
Creative Thinking Idea Generation	Not Evident	Developing	Approaching	○ Meeting Target	Extending
Communication Expressiveness	Not Evident	Developing	Approaching	○ Meeting Target	Extending
Global Mindedness Empathy	Not Evident	Emerging	Developing	Developed	○ Highly Developed

FIGURE 4.9: Sample of integrated assessment feedback.

specific feedback on the numerous elements that contribute to success on the task. This feedback provides fodder for reflection and dialogue about the various goals and the levels to which the student demonstrated each one. It also supports data collection related to short- and long-term student achievement and growth.

This feedback structure also works well for schools and districts seeking to move toward a mastery approach to grading, reporting, and generating transcripts. The structure of learning goals and the use of similar scales mean that we can aggregate feedback and data around defined domains of mastery relatively easily.

The processes described in this chapter may look complex and time-consuming without a digital platform to manage assessment design, feedback, and data management. These tasks can be accomplished without such a platform, but schools should strongly consider digital tools that help facilitate the work and make use of the data. One such platform that I work with is LearningBoard (https://learningboard.co), which greatly simplifies and elevates the use of such an assessment and feedback approach. It allows teachers to select academic goals and integrate impacts into individual assessments using the school's library of standards and impact performance areas and indicators. This, in turn, creates a feedback template prepopulated with the scales for each assessment goal within the task. Teachers simply move sliders and add comments to record feedback for a specific student on the specific assessment task. The system also stores all feedback data so educators can view them over time, aggregate them, disaggregate them, report them, and communicate about student progress. As of 2019, most existing software (PowerSchool, Gradelink SIS, Alma, and GradeMaster, for example) is focused on standards-based grading and gradebook-like software. Many have been developed out of existing student information systems. Very few actually provide the ability to integrate academic standards and transdisciplinary learning goals at the assessment design and feedback level described.

Conclusion

This chapter has covered a lot of ground. Building on the clear articulation of impacts as demonstrable learning goals that chapter 3 (page 39) described, this chapter has explained how to design assessments for and gather evidence of impacts and their performance areas. We also explored providing feedback to students and gathering useful data to assess whether educators and organizations are truly helping students achieve these mission-centered goals. In the next chapter, we will discuss using the I-O-I framework to drive innovation and focus strategic efforts.

Chapter 4 Resources

School and district teams can use the following questions and activities to put the concepts from this chapter into action. Teams should retain artifacts resulting from these exercises to inform later work.

Collaborative Inquiry

Consider the following questions, then discuss your answers as a team.

- What types of learning goals are represented in our mission, vision, and other core documents?
- How might we sort our performance areas into the suggested categories of cognitive skills and dispositions?
- How might you explain the benefits of the scale structure applied to impact performance areas and indicators? How might you answer concerns?
- How much consistency do we currently have in the ways we provide assessment feedback on academic goals?
- What hurdles might we face in implementing consistent scales across the grades and subject areas?

Collaborative Activities

The following activities will help you and your team operationalize the ideas from this chapter. Each activity builds on the one before it, so we recommend completing them in the order shown. Be sure to review the instructions in advance and gather any needed materials, such as markers and chart paper.

Put It to the Test

Gather a few pieces of evidence of student learning that address various performance areas, both cognitive skills and dispositions. In small groups of three or four, agree on what your look-for would be for each artifact. Each small group should examine the same artifact. Have each group member individually use the applicable performance area's sliding scale to provide feedback on the level to which the artifact demonstrates the desired learning.

Bring the small group back together to share and discuss the group members' placement of feedback on the scale. Use the following questions to help with the dialogue.

- Why did you place the slider where you did?
- What kept you from placing it higher or lower on the scale?
- How would you explain your feedback to the student?

Complete the activity by identifying the benefits and challenges of using such a framework to assess student success at demonstrating impacts' performance areas.

Communicate, Communicate, Communicate

Break the team into four small groups, if you have the numbers to do so. If not, work with all the team members throughout the activity. Their task is to come up with a brief presentation (two or three PowerPoint slides, for instance) that will communicate the feedback structure to the following audiences.

- Students
- Parents
- Teachers
- The school board or governing body

Each small group would create the presentation for one constituent group. Keep the communication focused and brief. You may want to use the why-what-how structure to frame your messaging.

Focus on Data

We are used to creating data teams around more standardized assessment data, such as reading or mathematics scores on common tests. We're also familiar with how these teams should address the observations and insights they derive from their inquiry into these data. Traditionally, small data teams will gather to inquire into the data, note positive or negative data or trends, hypothesize as to why these might exist, and agree on a course of action to correct a perceived issue. How might we do something similar for impacts?

Brainstorm the ways in which you might structure team moderation of artifacts and evidence of impacts so you develop consistent interpretation and application of impact scales. How might you bring educators together to interpret evidence of learning through this lens?

Finally, how might data teams use the data collected through this assessment framework to make observations, derive insights, and plan to address learning in impact areas? How might educators delve into the data from both a narrow and a broad perspective? What role might students play in interpreting evidence?

Integrated Feedback Template

	Insufficient Evidence	Not Meeting	Approaching	Meeting	Exemplary			
Academic Goals								
Impact Performance Areas (Cognitive Skills)	Not Evident	Developing	Approaching	Meeting Target	Extending			
Impact Performance Areas (Dispositions)	Not Evident	Emerging	Developing	Developed	Highly Developed			

CHAPTER 5

HOW
Designing Systems Around Impacts

Activating the I-O-I framework is where most of the transformation occurs, but we cannot achieve this activation without building the foundation that the prior chapters outline. To this point, we have worked through a structured process to set the stage for innovation and transformation. Now we can leverage that essential foundational work to catalyze lasting change. The processes we will explore in this chapter are not implementation actions; they are strategies that will help you enact your long-term goals for learning. As described in chapter 1 (page 14), traditional strategic plans that list static implementation steps are inappropriate for modern educational systems. The modern strategic approach is more about strategic thinking and action planning than about creating a binder full of documents.

In this chapter, we will discuss developing catalysts for change and structuring strategic thinking efforts in service of impacts. The premise is simple, yet it can have profound effects. The central question of this chapter is, How do we focus our strategic thinking and organizational efforts on achieving our impacts? In response, we'll explore tools and strategies for impacts, the implications for systems, the implications for learning, and matters related to a visual model of the learning environment.

Tools and Strategies for Impacts

As we think backward in order to align what students should learn beyond content, let's explore what this might mean in the case of an impact-focused instructional environment. As performance areas and indicators become a focus of the instructional system, we must provide students with tools and strategies that help them put impacts into practice. These tools and strategies allow teachers to intentionally support students in becoming adept in the performance areas and activating them to be successful learners. We would never assess students' ability to solve quadratic equations without first teaching it to them. The same holds true for impacts. The effect of defining tools (specifically designed implements, like a template or software) and strategies (targeted processes, like a procedure or technique) for impacts actually moves us beyond content and toward modern learning. We can expand our notion of content to include tools and strategies aligned with impacts' performance areas.

Including tools and strategies in your curriculum design and delivery also supports teachers who will—rightly—say that they are not trained in teaching creative thinking, for example, or other impacts. Providing teachers with an accessible set of tools and strategies for a performance area of an impact helps them introduce concrete methodologies and processes that students can use to demonstrate skills and dispositions. It also creates consistency across subject areas. For example, a school can introduce a common problem-solving process that students can learn and utilize in any class. Additionally, by aligning these tools with the grade-band levels of performance indicators, we can build students' capabilities purposefully, increasing the level of sophistication and complexity over time.

As with performance indicators, we should not see these tools and strategies as prescriptive or restrictive. Teachers should not merely check off that a student uses a tool or strategy, but rather interpret the level to which a student utilizes it to demonstrate the desired performance area within a task's context. We have many examples of appropriate tools and strategies to choose from. Figure 5.1 provides an example of what tools and strategies might look like for one impact area. In this high-school level example, the impact is critical thinking, and its performance areas include inquiry, analysis, and resolution. A school can start with a small number of strategies and let the set grow organically. Indeed, many teachers will have tools and strategies that they could and should add to this resource. In a digital learning management system, all the tools and strategies listed could link to the actual resources.

	Critical Thinking		
	Inquiry	**Analysis**	**Resolution**
Performance Indicators	Students can: • Generate questions for complex problems and concepts • Connect prior knowledge and understanding as a starting point to understanding concepts and ideas • Collect and collate primary data appropriate to research questions • Access information using well-designed search strategies • Independently use a range of formats and modes to seek, access, and use information • Organize information in logical and coherent ways • Read for meaning and understanding connected to the topic being researched • Research and begin to form a critique of an existing work that shows they are starting to understand the personal context	Students can: • Identify patterns, similarities, and differences in information • Identify bias and limitations within information and data • Connect and extend knowledge and information from various sources • Interpret information from various viewpoints • Organize information to show understandings • Create a works-cited list to organize and recognize sources • Make accurate inferences based on data and information • Critically evaluate sources for authority, currency, accuracy, and relevance • Evaluate the meaning of the text, themes, and ideas the author presents • Critically and contextually analyze the meaning of past, present, and emerging information • Understand analysis techniques in order to deduce, infer, and communicate possible logical meanings from different contexts	Students can: • Draw conclusions or state solutions based on research and understandings • Justify ideas based on research and understandings • Present multiple perspectives on an issue, idea, or topic • Explain potential consequences of solutions • Select from a range of alternative viewpoints • Cite others' ideas to support their own

FIGURE 5.1: Performance indicators and associated tools and strategies for critical thinking, high school.

continued ⇨

Tools and Strategies	• Venn diagrams, plus a lesson plan and example, and mind maps • Problem-solving strategies wheel • Research strategies • Research tools • Guess-check-improve method	• Various visual strategies for information organization, plus some resources • Information literacy tools • Information organization tools • Large source of problem-solving strategies • Deductive reasoning activity • Inductive reasoning lesson • Abductive reasoning activity	• Strategy for checking for bias • Strategies for drawing conclusions • Strategy for exploring the intended and possible unintended consequences of solutions

This is a simple yet powerful example of how we might drive change backward from impacts to enrich the content we teach. While many educators are rightfully concerned about the amount of content contained in academic standards, impacts are those cognitive skills and dispositions that help students become better learners, resulting in more success within academic subject areas. Also, many sets of academic standards, such as the Next Generation Science Standards (NGSS Lead States, 2013) and the College, Career, and Civic Life (C3) Framework for Social Studies State Standards (National Council for the Social Studies, 2013), explicitly include cognitive skills and other 21st century learning goals.

Implications for Systems

A *system* is any working structure within educational organizations for which we use a specific term: assessment, grading, reporting, communication, recruitment, leadership, professional learning, appraisal, culture, and so on. Driving change backward—from the end goal to the first step—through all systems of a learning organization is a main design principle of I-O-I. In fact, this book centers on the premise that pushing sporadic and isolated change initiatives first does not work and instead creates negative busyness and stymies progress. By contrast, the backward approach can create a sort of gravitational pull that draws other systems within the organization into orbit in a more organic and holistic way. Schools that truly use the I-O-I framework experience its powerful effects on each of their many systems.

As an example, consider assessment. Many schools and districts have tried to update assessment practice inputs first—where an assessment committee researches best practice in assessment design, labors over a document, publishes the document, and asks people to follow it. This approach never seems to achieve much except, perhaps, more busyness. Why is that? It's because it usually doesn't change the learning goals we are assessing. Educators could still administer traditional assessments and get what they need to give a grade and, eventually, fill in a report card. Why would educators change the way they assess if they are still responsible for assessing the same things? When initiatives or change are pushed into an educational organization, the organizational culture usually pushes it right back out again (or at least dilutes it so the effect is negligible).

On the other hand, if we commit to establishing impacts first and elevating them alongside academic goals, we need to collect evidence and provide feedback for that evidence, which makes it impossible to *not* change traditional assessment practice. We need to assess these new, clearly articulated learning goals. In order to assess them, we need to create opportunities for students to demonstrate them. Most traditional forms of assessment don't provide that opportunity, so we design new ones. The impact learning goals compel us to realign our assessment practices—and they similarly affect each and every system in the school.

Our commitment to truly embed impacts drives the need for change. Schools are resistant to change and have a tendency to reject or ignore what is pushed into their environment. But in the case of I-O-I, the need for change becomes self-evident, and systems, with the right leadership and prompting, will seek alignment with that strong, core goal.

Exploring the larger implications of our simple premise gives us a great way to look at how all systems within an educational organization might align with and contribute to common strategic goals for learning. We can frame the premise quite simply: our goal is to help students achieve impacts by elevating them alongside academic learning goals, capturing and interpreting evidence, and embedding impacts within our definition of successful learning in all that we do. What implications might this have for all our schools' systems?

Schools can engage various groups to investigate this implication question for all systems within a school: assessment, grading, reporting, professional learning, hiring, communication, finance, yearly goal setting, board reporting, culture, physical spaces, professional evaluation, classroom observations, schedules, and so on. In this way, educators can begin to define the path of each system, as well as the systems' interdependence, as the systems come into orbit around the central goal or mission as articulated through impacts. Often, the interdependence of these systems is overlooked or underexplored. There is no magic bullet to achieving a transformational change, and organizations need to think strategically about how to make sure each system supports the goal in its own way. The whole is truly larger than the sum of its parts when it comes to leading transformation. I have frequently witnessed the misalignment of one system (professional learning or reporting, for example) with another system that is leading the transformation (new learning goals for assessment feedback, for example). The result is almost always confusion and, ultimately, the erosion of transformation efforts.

As one example, the School District of Greenfield's G21 impacts design team investigated the implications for its schools. The district's process highlights implication deep dives as engaging but efficient ways to think backward. After introducing the premise that everything should begin with impacts and the implication question, the design team divided into smaller groups of two or three people. In these groups, members considered the implications for assessment and framed their responses with the sentence stem, "This means _____." The smaller groups took fifteen minutes to brainstorm and come up with five or so insights. Each group shared responses, and the team culled those into the rough list shown in figure 5.2.

This means:
- Not everything will receive a grade
- Portfolios to demonstrate growth over time
- Applying common criteria for interpreting different artifacts
- Process is central
- Students will receive useful feedback to inform goal setting, strengths, and so on
- Assessment is the beginning of a process, not the end
- Students will be part of assessment design and feedback
- Assessment will be performance based and require transferable elements
- Assessment will be ongoing, revisable, not all at the same time
- Assessment will be interdisciplinary
- Assessment will be based on what students demonstrate and not what they don't
- Student voice and choice (individual requests for focus)
- Clear expectations
- All feedback comes from learning
- Growth will be demonstrated in an ongoing way
- Assessment is feedback

Source: © 2017 by School District of Greenfield, 2017. Used with permission.

FIGURE 5.2: Brainstormed list of implications for assessment.

These responses included very rough phrases that simply captured initial insights. The team took these phrases and tweaked them to create more defined principles to guide assessments, as shown in figure 5.3.

- Assessment design is goal based, not task based, and artifacts can vary.
- Assessment design should match tasks with the learning goals to be assessed.
- Contemporary assessment design includes elements of process as well as product.
- Students have voice and choice in assessment design, products, and, where appropriate, criteria.
- Performance-based and transfer tasks are the most authentic forms of rich assessment design for both academic and G21 impact goals.
- G21 impact elements should be brought alongside academic goals where these elements are important to student success in specific tasks.
- Assessment design should be flexible and personalized (in time, place, and format).
- Authentic assessment design involves elements from multiple disciplines.
- Assessment designs should seek to capture what students understand and can do, not what they don't or can't.

Source: © 2017 by School District of Greenfield. Used with permission.

FIGURE 5.3: Sample assessment principles resulting from an implication deep dive.

The idea was not to create yet another document but to explore, think through, and articulate insights to bring assessment practices into alignment with impact goals. This has led to rich assessment design, assessment review sessions, professional learning, and a myriad of other ways that the district might shift its assessment design and practices in the service of impacts. As Patrice Ball, director of secondary education, states, "Focusing on the impacts has helped us contemporize our entire system" (P. Ball, personal communication, July 8, 2018).

Implication deep dives can take place in similar ways with all systems. It is not practical to dive into them all at once; rather, schools should prioritize the immediate systems that will build momentum for significant and continued change. Usually, core systems such as assessment, curriculum design, reporting, and professional learning will come first, followed by systems a little further out from the center. As you begin the process, you will see other systems, such as athletics, professional appraisal, and service learning, seek alignment as well.

>
> We must stop:
> - Rushing to big actions and gestures before building a thoughtful foundation
> - Rushing ahead without pausing to explore, think, and collaborate
> - Ignoring the implications of one shift on other systems
> - Thinking of change as isolated and singular

Implications for Learning

In addition to shifting a school's distinct systems, I-O-I also permits and necessitates different approaches to learning. I-O-I promotes change and innovation in how a school selects programmatic approaches to learning because the school must intentionally choose approaches that best service the impacts. We refer to these approaches to teaching and learning as the major *pathways* of the school's larger educational model. This ensures that teaching and learning structures—the how—such as project-based learning, student self-reporting, or a personalized mentoring program, are aligned in service of clear learning goals. As a backward design process, I-O-I desires to get away from the untethered cycles of implementation we often see in schools. When asked what they are currently doing, most schools can list the new initiatives or programs they are putting in place, but they can rarely articulate the purpose of these implementations. These implementations don't last, or schools don't fully implement them, for the same reason that efforts to reform assessment design often fail: the learning goals have not really changed. Before a school can choose pathways, however, educators must develop a shared understanding of how the school's learning environment needs to change.

Developing a Shared Understanding

To develop a shared understanding, schools should begin by questioning which approaches to teaching and learning will best help students develop and demonstrate impacts. At this stage, we want general descriptions, not program names. Instead of jumping to a named approach, such as makerspaces or personalized learning, teams should articulate the types and characteristics of the teaching and learning experience needed to achieve the larger goal. Similar to the construction of assessment design principles mentioned previously, simple descriptions follow from the implications of the transformational goals we seek. We may say that in order to develop the impact of self-directed learning, students must be able to have a voice in what they learn, how they learn it, and how they demonstrate their learning. If we wish students to develop creative problem solving, we may say that engaging in real-world learning experiences outside of the school environment is one of the best ways to do this. In the end, most teams I have worked with realize that what is needed cannot be defined by the name of one program, but represents a number of shifts that, together, create a climate, culture, and ecosystem for the learning they seek. Elements may be pulled from several programs as are best suited to creating this dynamic environment. And, usually, teams will come to understand that they have most of the tools needed to achieve this and clearly articulate any areas of need.

The school team should consider and articulate the type of learning environment that it envisions will help deliver its goals. The team first needs to articulate this desired state before it can decide which pathway has the greatest potential to get it there. Articulating this desired state doesn't have to be a long process. The desired output of this process is not another document but a shared understanding about what the team believes will help students perform and grow in areas of impact.

Choosing Pathways

With the guidance of a shared understanding, now the team can select pathways. When making this selection, the team must use the descriptors from the shared understanding to assess the programmatic approaches that may facilitate the achievement of learning goals. We need to assess the appropriateness of major programmatic approaches against that foundational understanding.

The school team functions here as a design team. Using the descriptors of the shared understanding, they can now explore various programs to see which have elements that will support the desired shifts. The group may come up with a set of pathways that uses certain elements of the project-based learning program from a specific organization, an apprenticeship program drawn largely from a second group, an approach to portfolios and goal setting borrowed from another district, the global education framework designed by a university professor, and so on. No single program is going to fit perfectly and create transformative change on its own. An intelligent and creative design process can, however, identify the supporting sources for elements of the desired and necessary environment for learning. A school's education system is like a tapestry, and each major thread is a pathway.

These pathways represent the outputs within the I-O-I parlance. They are strategies selected to achieve the organization's long-term transformational goals for learning.

Inputs (actions and resources) will need to be planned in order to realize the outputs. And, they cannot all be implemented at once. We will further explore the planning of outputs and inputs in chapter 6.

Teams often realize that, while the observations and characteristics they identify as the desired learning environment may be shared by the big programmatic movements of the day, they do not represent a single established program. Instead, they represent a number of shifts that teams can accomplish internally.

There is no singular approach to or silver bullet for transformation, but schools have clear and identifiable shifts they can make over time—their pathways—to create the desired learning environment. For many educators, this is a liberating realization. They no longer need to search for a needle in a haystack—instead, they have found their box of needles in a drawer. Rather than program shopping, educators must empower themselves to act on these shifts internally.

We must stop:
- Searching for a silver bullet to transform our organizations
- Shopping for educational trends
- Doing things that no longer align with our newly articulated goals
- Enabling or participating in binary arguments that pit academic content against impacts

A Visual Model of the Learning Environment

Once a school team has selected a few key pathways, the team can synthesize a cohesive visual model of the learning environment. A visual model is an excellent tool that can communicate the relationships between core elements of a learning environment. Such models bring all the pieces together into a simple representation of what is, in fact, a fairly complex structure. Educators can point to the visual as "our model" and can explain it clearly.

As one example, I worked with the International School of Kenya (ISK) in Nairobi to develop an exemplary visual model. Figure 5.4 displays the school's visual model.

How: Designing Systems Around Impacts 91

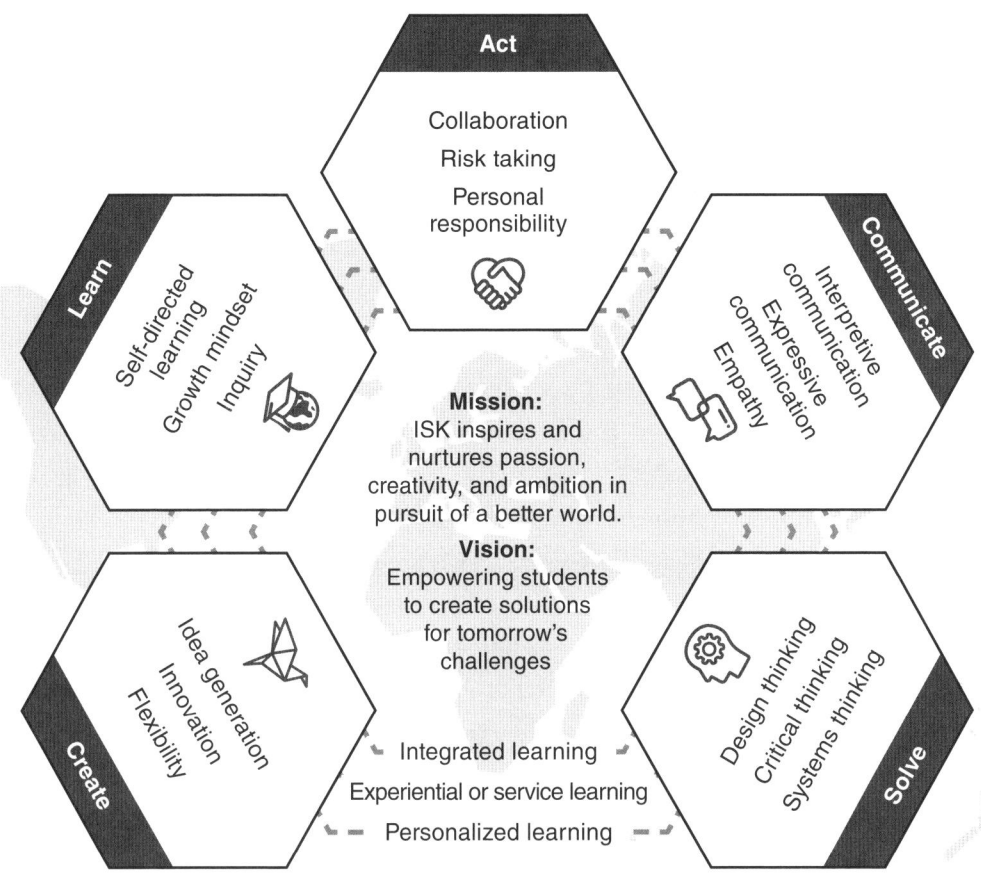

Source: © 2017 by International School of Kenya. Used with permission.

FIGURE 5.4: Sample visual model of a learning environment.

This diagram is clear, interconnected, and simple. ISK's mission and vision statements appear in the center. Around these statements, in the hexagons, are the school's impacts, each of which lists several related performance areas. The three major pathways that the school chose—(1) integrated learning, (2) experiential or service learning, and (3) personalized learning—connect the impacts. The school chose these pathways as the programmatic approaches most likely to help its students achieve the specific impacts and performance areas. Notably, the pathways are not dominating programs you need to purchase; rather, they are manners of teaching and learning that can develop over time. In fact, ISK had already been developing these three pathways, and the model gave the school something to target (impacts) in its further development and implementation. The pathways in the model were not isolated innovations but a suite of approaches that served clear goals for learning.

A visual model such as this can also be seen through the I-O-I lens. The impacts and their performance areas are clearly articulated. The pathways represent the major programmatic outputs and the strategies for achieving the impacts. Finally, these all surround the mission and vision in support of achieving them. A model such as this can represent the organization's strategic plan for teaching and learning in a concise way, with inputs being planned as part of yearly goal setting and planning.

Conclusion

In this chapter, we have explored ways in which educational systems can align with impacts (long-term learning goals at the heart of the mission). With some intentional consideration on educators' part, a relentless pursuit of impacts will have positive implications for different systems within the organization. And exploring those implications will help us understand how we can align each system with the high-level goal of achieving impacts. We can find a way to bring these systems into orbit around our goal so that we create a cohesive environment. Finally, these explorations can lead us to conceive of a model of the desired learning environment, which includes the major programmatic shifts we would like to make in service of our goals. This model should tie everything together and provide the blueprint for future strategic thinking and action planning. It also provides us with ample opportunities to identify strategic actions as we work to enact the model. In the next chapter, we will focus on the final how of school change, facilitating change by implementing the I-O-I framework.

Chapter 5 Resources

School and district teams can use the following questions and activities to put the concepts from this chapter into action. Teams should retain artifacts resulting from these exercises to inform later work.

Collaborative Inquiry

Consider the following questions, then discuss your answers as a team.

- Besides the idea of systems being pulled into alignment by the gravity of impacts, what analogy might help us and others understand elements of complex environments?
- Why do we think past change initiatives may not have stuck or reached their potential?
- How would you describe the difference between driving change backward and pushing plan implementation first?
- If a teacher stated, "I can't do impacts because I have so much content to cover," how might you respond?
- Which systems would you prioritize for our first implication deep dives? What other systems would follow?

Collaborative Activities

The following activities will help you and your team operationalize the ideas from this chapter. Each activity builds on the one before it, so we recommend completing them in the order shown. Be sure to review the instructions in advance and gather any needed materials, such as markers and chart paper.

Diving Into Implications

As this chapter described, an implication deep dive gives groups a great way to engage in strategic thinking; also, groups can use the output of their deep dive (the resulting worksheet, page 96) to frame future strategic thinking and actions. The following deep dive process should take no longer than forty-five minutes. After the first deep dive, experienced groups can complete deep dives more quickly, especially when they focus on generating ideas (as opposed to getting caught up in the minute details). Consider the following steps.

1. Create groups of no more than four.
2. Ask each group to choose a system. A system is a working structure within educational organizations for which we use a specific term: *assessment*, *grading*, *reporting*, *communication*, *recruitment*, *leadership*, *professional learning*, *appraisal*, *culture*, and so on.
3. Ask each group to discuss the system and make sure that the members have a shared understanding about what that system involves.

4. Have the groups read the premise and ponder it quietly for a minute or two. The premise could also be projected for the whole group so that everyone can read it individually.

5. Distribute the worksheet for this activity (page 96). Ask the groups to start brainstorming and building a list of implications that impacts have on that system. At this stage, groups simply look to briefly capture each idea—without worrying about writing complete sentences.

6. Have them consolidate, sort, prioritize, and group these ideas and create short statements that represent the main ideas. They may group several implications and create a single insight statement for them. The goal is to arrive at a smaller number of statements that articulate the way in which the premise should affect that system.

7. Groups should come together to review, discuss, and agree on the implications articulated.

Creating the Desired Learning Environment

As stated in the chapter, we need to understand the change we seek before we try to select any programs. We have done this with impacts, but we also need to do this for the learning environment itself. What type of learning environment will best support students and teachers in achieving our highest goals for learning?

This activity has groups list the qualities of the shifts they believe will support their strategic direction. Again, staying out of the distracting details is important at this stage. A process like this can easily be muddied by side commentary, personal anecdotes, and so on. Skillful facilitation is a must. Consider the following steps.

1. Make sure the members involved in this activity are familiar with the organization's impacts and strategic direction. The greater their engagement in these, the more the members will align their vision of a desired future learning environment to them.

2. Divide the members into groups of no more than four people.

3. Ask groups to share what they think focusing on impacts and elevating them alongside academic goals mean in general terms.

4. Ask groups to envision the type of learning environment that they would expect to see when the organization has successfully achieved its strategic learning goals. What would that desired and necessary future environment look like? What would they hear? What would they feel?

5. Groups should record their "future observations" on pieces of poster paper. They should avoid inert language and focus on observable factors.

6. After twenty minutes or so of brainstorming, post all the pieces of poster paper around the room. Simply ask people to do a gallery walk and put a mark beside the observations they feel are important and representative of that desired future environment.

7. Bring these common and endorsed observations back to the larger group. Perhaps cut them out from the posters and physically group like observations. Groups could sort them into student actions and educator actions, for example.

8. Once they have done a rough sorting, ask the group to develop a brief characteristic statement that represents the core of the observation or group of observations. What principles might drive the design and maintenance of such an environment?

The following chart shows sample results of this activity. These results would inform the next step of choosing the programmatic approaches (or elements of these approaches) the organization may want to use to build this desired future learning environment.

Observations	Characteristics
• Students moving about the building and interacting with different adults • Students accessing materials (markers, sticky notes, cardboard, and tape) to generate and share ideas with others • Some students working alone and some working with a group • Impact tools and strategies posted or readily available • Pieces of projects and prototypes everywhere • Students seeking and recording feedback from adults and peers • Time set aside for students to contribute artifacts to their portfolios, self-assess, and write reflections	• The schedule allows for all students and adults to pursue projects. • There is a high level of self-directed learning. • Innovation and collaboration (different groupings) are central. • Students understand and use design processes. • Feedback is regular, recorded, and acted on. • Student self-assessment is valued.

Implication Deep Dive Worksheet

Premise: Our goal is to help students achieve impacts by elevating them alongside academic learning goals and embedding them in our definition of successful learning. What implications does that have for our educational systems?

System	Implications This means _____.	Insights and Understandings
Grading		
Reporting		
Board Reporting		
Professional Learning		
Other		

CHAPTER 6
HOW
Facilitating Change

In this chapter, we will return to the premise that traditional strategic planning has not been the proper approach to transformation. Perhaps it even inadvertently stifled well-intentioned change efforts. The goal of traditional strategic planning (an input) was to create a strategic plan (an output). We then followed the script laid out in the plan, full of activities (more inputs) and documents (outputs generated by those inputs). We all stayed very busy focusing on what the organization was doing.

But we largely left out student learning, especially when it came to measuring the success of our strategic plan. We often measured success only by the completion of the plan's inputs and outputs. If we completed the steps of the plan, we could put a big green check mark in that box. Schools would say that they started with their mission when they developed a strategic plan, and this is largely true. Their measures of success, however, very rarely related to this mission. According to traditional strategic planning, we believed that if we did A and B, C would just happen in a linear and causal way—if we developed a service learning program, all students would become global citizens. We believed this to such a degree that we often neglected to define what C looked like and what evidence would demonstrate its achievement. C was often just an aspiration or mission statement on a wall. We pointed to it every once in a while, but rarely enacted it in a demonstrable, assessable way. Lisa Elliott, superintendent of the School District of Greenfield in Greenfield, Wisconsin, describes the problem: "The previous strategic plan consisted of many initiatives and lists of adult-centered actions; however, there was not a clear focus on what student outcomes were to be elicited as a result of the adult actions" (L. Elliott, personal communication, July 9, 2018).

To summarize:

- **Static strategic plans exist in a past age of assumed predictability and control**—Besides the fact that most strategic plans are created by looking at data from the past rather than insights of the future, it is illogical to write down five years' worth of inputs and outputs and carry them out with no adjustment. It's not only impossible but unhelpful to try to plan for five years from now.
- **Static strategic plans trap us in the input-output cycle**—We often approach traditional strategic plans with the goal of finishing the plan. But our goal is not to simply carry out the plan; our goal is to achieve and demonstrate our mission. In the absence of clear and measurable impacts, implementation steps dominate strategic plans. Without impacts, we can only measure success by the fact that the plan *was* implemented. We cannot drive transformation if we have no clarity on what we are transforming into and no real measures to see if the change has benefited students and the mission.

Thus far, this book has outlined ways in which we can build a mission-centered foundation by identifying essential future-focused impact learning goals that represent our mission. In this chapter, we will describe possible ways in which we can use I-O-I and its potential to drive transformation. Our driving question is, How do we structure and evaluate the change process based on I-O-I? In response, we will explore the following topics: strategic oversight and facilitation, preparation for change, a rolling strategic process, an implementation timeline, and two tracks of accountability.

Strategic Oversight and Facilitation

The type of iterative approach to change that this chapter describes has many moving parts; this necessitates some sort of strategic facilitation team (SFT). In the past, we may have thought of this as a strategic planning committee that went away for the weekend and wrote a traditional strategic plan. In a modern environment, this team would comprise thought leaders representing various constituencies (students, parents, teachers, leadership, board members, the business community, postsecondary educators, a teacher-training college, and so on). The broad membership engages more people in the change process. This team should be interested, facilitated, and regularly active to provide strategic leadership and oversight. In short, the members' tasks should be to:

- Develop elements of the initial strategic document as a concise statement of goals and major strategic initiatives (often related to pathways)
- Request resources, especially to fund elements of the rolling strategic process
- Frame the goals that will enter the rolling strategic process
- Develop, review, and propose actions for the upcoming year
- Establish, review, and interpret measures of success for impacts
- Report yearly to the board and the community on progress and success at achieving goals
- Contribute relevant evidence and data to accreditation or compliance processes

The size and makeup of this team should reflect the organization's context. Also, this team needs to consider and harness the talents of people across the organization. Too often, a small group of people try to take on all the work. This is unsustainable and wastes organizational and community capabilities. I-O-I is a structure where everyone does something, but no one does everything. Having the right people doing the right things will help immensely. Groups should be carefully constructed according to their purpose and the capacities needed for them to function effectively. For example, an SFT would benefit from a broad collective skillset, including members experienced in change leadership, resource planning, communication, pedagogy, governance, innovation, and so on. By creating multiple opportunities for growth and leadership, the SFT will show its commitment to developing impacts and help create the sort of positive, collaborative culture that is both desired as an outcome and needed for success.

Preparation for Change

To get ready to implement the rolling strategic process, it is essential that the SFT clearly define its goals. In the next two sections, we will discuss writing effective goal statements and breaking down larger goals into inputs and outputs.

Goal Statements

As mentioned previously, it is important that goals are clearly articulated so that the true target of the goal and, therefore, valid evidence of success are understood by all stakeholders. The learning goals must be first and foremost, not the organizational inputs or outputs. This keeps a school focused and helps the team develop appropriate learning-focused types and sources of evidence.

In chapter 3 (page 40), we discussed the need to develop an informed view of the future in order to identify and articulate impacts. The same holds true for generating these more specific goal statements. For example, the impact may be to develop students with the skills and dispositions of global-minded citizens. The SFT, through its work, may suggest embedding global issues into the curriculum and redesigning the approach to service learning as a starting point to accomplish this impact goal. So, the goal statement might be, "To develop and improve our students' global mindedness through service learning and the infusion of global issues into the curriculum." Note that when goals are written in this format, "every teacher in every content area can see the application to his or her classroom" (L. Elliott, personal communication, June 8, 2018).

Notice that the goal is related to student learning and, specifically, impacts. The goal is not to create a new service learning program or embed global issues into the curriculum. The SFT has chosen these as the vehicles to achieve the goal of improving students' global mindedness. The key difference comes when we choose our evidence of success. If our goal were to develop a new service learning program, what would our evidence of success be? Simply that we did it. If our goal is to develop and improve our students' global mindedness, what evidence of success will we choose? Learning evidence related to our articulated look-fors interpreted through our related scales. This stress on learning-focused evidence makes a world of difference. It demands that you look at what learning is really happening and hold yourself accountable to your mission.

Inputs and Outputs

Goal statements provide direction, but inputs and outputs are the series of steps the school takes along the way. Educational organizations are pretty good at planning inputs and outputs. In fact, traditional strategic plans are full of them, and often not much else. Because educators are so familiar with them, this book has primarily focused on the transformational potential of impacts. Inputs and outputs simply give us a way to break down the bigger goals and the work we will undertake to achieve them. Figure 6.1 shows an example of how to plan outputs and inputs based on an impact goal.

Outputs	Inputs
Impact goal statement: To develop and improve our students' global mindedness through service learning and the infusion of global issues into the curriculum	
Build a knowledge base.	• Assemble a design team. • Train the design team. • Carry out research. • Carry out school visits (funding required). • Consolidate the knowledge base.
Design a potential solution.	• Carry out design sessions. • Design a solution. • Check the early design. • Refine the design. • Identify goals and evidence needed from the prototyping process.
Refine the solution.	• Develop mechanisms for capturing feedback and evidence from the prototyping process. • Decide on an evidence analysis protocol. • Seek willing prototypers. • Orient the prototypers. • Start the prototyping process. • Start capturing evidence. • Analyze evidence and decide on its implications for design. • Debrief with the prototypers. • Complete the refined design.
Develop inputs and outputs for the execution phase.	• Have planning sessions to prepare an action plan for year 1 of execution. • Informally share with divisional or site-based leadership. • Revise, complete, and submit an input-output action plan.
Establish evidence of success.	• Review the suitability of evidence collected from the prototyping process, and assess these measures' suitability as a long-term measure (you will be using them to assess improvement). • Refine with possible look-fors and look-ats. • Add to the suggested action plan for next year, and submit it.

FIGURE 6.1: Input-output planning for impacts.

Most planning documents would also include columns for who is responsible for each task or input, projected completion dates, and any possible resources needed for each input. Figure 6.1 (page 101) is a broad example, but it represents the work needed for a worthwhile iteration of the rolling strategic process. Regardless of the desired outputs and inputs, we need to plan in a clear, linear fashion to support the work. Also, the action plan should:

- Keep to a relatively short time horizon
- Include both processes (inputs) and products (outputs)
- Group inputs within outputs to provide direction without subdividing too much
- Form the basis of a checklist for monitoring and supporting progress and completing the action plan

A communication plan should also accompany this sort of input-output action plan. We often overlook communication or assume it will take care of itself—you may have experienced how quickly this assumption can derail the best-laid plans. Schools and districts should think about which elements of the action plan to communicate to various audiences, the core message behind that communication, who should communicate with those audiences, and how and when they should communicate. Time spent on this can save a great deal of time later on. The easiest fire to put out is one you prevent in the first place. Strategic communication planning can be a big help in this area.

We must stop:

- Confusing action planning (the means) and goal setting (the ends)
- Developing goals focused on the achievement of outputs only
- Believing that the goal of strategic thinking is a traditional strategic plan
- Tracking and measuring only inputs and outputs
- Isolating strategic thinking and design outside of our day-to-day work

Rolling Strategic Process

With the aforementioned preparations in place, a school is ready to enact a rolling strategic process for change. For this book, we will define *rolling strategic process* as an adaptive, iterative process for achieving long-term transformational goals for learning (impacts). It creates a pattern of strategic thinking and action that is driven by organizational learning and design. A rolling strategic process does not mean making things up along the way or veering wildly across the educational landscape. The following principles form the foundation of the rolling strategic process.

- Strategic thinking takes time, and the organization must regularly engage its members as participants in strategic thinking.
- The organization selects strategies and actions based on collaborative learning and design.
- Strategies naturally evolve and have several phases in their life cycle.
- Defining a rolling strategic process provides a predictable and actionable path that the organization can follow across the life cycle of strategies.
- Strategies must be spread out, not implemented at the same time, so that the organization can work effectively and make use of all learning acquired throughout the process without being overloaded by trying too much at once.
- The organization's work with a strategy does not end once it has completed implementing the strategy. The organization must analyze evidence that tells it whether that strategy is contributing to the achievement of impacts.

To illustrate the phases of strategies' life cycle, we might envision the rolling strategic process as a cycle of steps that engage with each other, as shown in figure 6.2 (page 104). In the following sections, we will explore each phase in detail. Table 6.1 (page 104) briefly describes the phases of a rolling strategic process and provides examples of corresponding actions.

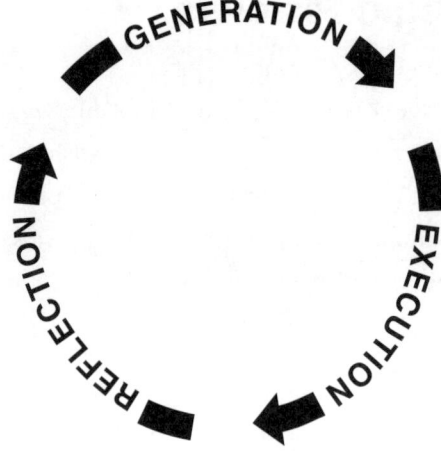

FIGURE 6.2: Rolling strategic process gears.

Table 6.1: Descriptions of the Phases of the Rolling Strategic Process

Phase	Description	Examples of Actions Within a Phase
Generation	Where the design team conceives a design and a strategy to achieve impacts, develops the strategy, and prepares for implementation	• Futures thinking • Research and knowledge base building • Design team work • Prototyping • Goal setting • Action planning • Community engagement
Execution	Where the design team leads the organization in implementing the strategy	• Communication • Change leadership • Professional learning • Resourcing and customization • Implementation
Reflection	Where the design team reviews the strategy based on evidence of achievement of impacts, and refines, redesigns, or rejects the strategy	• Evidence collection • Evidence interpretation • Strategy assessment • Action planning

Generation

Generation begins with a strategic needs-based goal. When a goal enters the generation phase, the school should form a design team for that goal. This allows dedicated time for proper strategic thinking and also offers a great opportunity to engage a broader perspective. Design teams offer important avenues to engage people through more focused involvement in an area of interest. While the SFT takes a broader perspective, design teams have a much more specific task that allows team members to go deeply into new areas and collaborate to create solutions that will work for their context. In my experience, teacher leaders often feel that design team membership provides them with a voice and some ownership over the direction of the organization. Design teams are much more than committees—they meet over a period of time, focus on learning first, carry out research and collaborative learning tasks, and essentially design a solution best suited to achieving their goal. That solution might involve designing a specific program or shift needed to address the goal, proposing updates to physical spaces, identifying new methodologies, using digital tools, or a combination of all of these.

The design team must properly prototype its solution. Prototyping is *not* piloting. It requires more than simply trying something out and getting anecdotal feedback. Prototyping is substantive and based on evidence that aligns with the goal. If the school is going to decide whether to implement the solution more broadly, it needs evidence that the innovation will achieve its stated goal. Imagine a school is considering investing hundreds of thousands of dollars and dozens of teacher-training hours to install interactive whiteboards in all classrooms. A typical pilot program might involve a few teachers trying out the technology, with the leadership deciding to fully implement interactive whiteboards because most of the teachers say that they like them. Clearly, this is not enough evidence to know whether this innovation is worth the time and money. A proper prototyping process would involve setting clear learning goals for the use of interactive whiteboards and collecting data to show whether their use can adequately meet those goals. Prototyping will allow the school to focus its efforts on innovations that have proven potential to help students achieve impacts. It will also build trust in the decision-making process and reduce busyness.

Prototyping provides a structured way to move beyond the busyness often associated with piloting a number of initiatives without a clear sense of what is being looked both for and at, in terms of the initiative's potential and appropriateness. It still takes time and energy, but that time and energy are likely to result in a more informed, transparent, and inclusive decision-making process. The innovations that move forward from the prototyping phase should be those that have proven that they deserve to spread in a sustainable fashion. Much of the feeling of busyness and disillusionment is based on the superficial ways in which we approach new initiatives and evidence-poor implementation planning that hinders sustainability.

The generation phase will result in something that the school can implement (a model, a program, or something similar) and a suggested action plan to guide the execution phase. In the rolling strategic processes described in this book, the action plan that the design team suggests will often go to divisional or school leadership teams, who will effectively carry out the plan in the execution phase. Strategic planning generally has two points of failure: (1) design flaws and (2) implementation flaws. A design flaw means that the solution proposed is not well researched or devised—the premise is flawed from the start. An implementation flaw means that something has gone wrong in the attempt to make the design a reality. The generation phase means that both design and implementation are considered carefully, thereby reducing flaws that will hinder overall success.

Execution

Schools often falter in the execution phase, largely because they have not done the proper thinking, designing, and prototyping work outlined in the generation phase, but also because they underestimate the complexity involved in successfully getting an innovation or change up and running. Execution is rarely as simple as following a list of steps. The overt, mechanical implementation steps (making the announcement, buying resources, training teachers, and so on) do not usually derail execution. Failure usually results from an inability to navigate complexity within learning communities. Most often, this stems from poor communication and ineffective change leadership.

Communication most often fails when leaders only communicate the what of the change and leave out the why and the how. Starting with the why is the obvious golden rule for communicating change. This must be achieved to establish a common purpose that the community (especially teachers) can get behind. Teachers, not unexpectedly, are then most interested in the how. The how is their daily reality. Shifting to the how is essential, but we should also consistently reinforce the why and what so that our communities can make the connection between what they are being asked to do or accept, the reasons behind this, and the model and designs that illustrate the bigger picture.

Effective change leadership involves setting the conditions in which the properties of the desired environment can emerge. It involves tending to necessary cultural shifts overtly and thoughtfully. It involves engaging the social-emotional considerations of all involved. Leaders must generate the positive energy that will tilt the environment toward success. They must anticipate potential unintended consequences and proactively address them. The details of skillful change leadership are beyond the scope of this book; for more information, readers can consult resources such as the following.

- *Nuance: Why Some Leaders Succeed and Others Fail* by Michael Fullan (2019)
- *Leadership on the Line: Staying Alive Through the Dangers of Change* by Ronald Heifetz and Marty Linsky (2017)
- *Immunity to Change: How to Overcome It and Unlock the Potential in Yourself and Your Organization* by Robert Kegan and Lisa Laskow Lahey (2009)
- *The Fifth Discipline: The Art and Practice of the Learning Organization* by Peter Senge (1994)
- *Change Leadership: A Practical Guide to Transforming Our Schools* by Tony Wagner and Robert Kegan (2006)

Reflection

Reflecting after implementing a new program seems like an obvious step, but often we minimize it or it lacks enough rigor to ensure accurate conclusions. We need to start by selecting the right evidence to assess whether the innovation has met its stated goals. Luckily, we set the goal and defined measures during the generation phase. The look-fors and look-ats for an impact goal also constitute evidence, as do the related feedback scales.

The design team captured and interpreted some baseline data as part of prototyping; for reflection, then, we need to capture and interpret similar evidence to see the change that resulted from implementation of the innovation. Finally, we should have data or evidence teams whose job it is to compare these data sets and assess the level to which the plan worked. The reflection phase should result in a conclusion on whether there is a link between goal achievement and implementation of the innovation. The data might also suggest refinement, redesign, or rejection of the innovation. Reflection is simple, but teams need to do it properly so that the school can focus its energies on what works, increase the success rate of all changes, and achieve its mission through impacts.

The reflection phase can feed the following vital information back into the generation phase.

- What works and what doesn't
- Lessons learned through design and implementation
- Unintended consequences
- Suggestions for further design
- Insights as to what future goal-setting efforts should include

The reflection stage does not necessarily mark the end of the road or the full achievement of the desired impacts. An initiative may be refined based on what was learned. The reflection may lead to the decision that the initiative is operational—doing what it was designed to—and has matured into common and sustained practice. Or, the school team may decide that there are new opportunities to explore in order to drive the impacts forward in new ways or that more work needs to be done in order to further transform learning in that area. In this case, the goal might cycle back into a new generation phase to take advantage of emerging opportunities or find another promising avenue for innovation. The point is that the process is dynamic and iterative, and it benefits from ongoing engagement, as Patrice Ball explains:

> The most visual effect [of the I-O-I framework] is through our school and district growth-planning process and products. They do not reside in binders alone any longer. The process is worth the time and effort, and the products inspire the hard work educators put in—knowing that the goal is enhancement of student learning. (P. Ball, personal communication, July 8, 2018)

Implementation Timeline

The rolling strategic process for each impact runs its course over several years. Impacts form the backbone of strategic thinking and action planning for years to come. They can be dealt with separately (each impact is a goal) or grouped; regardless, they provide clear destinations. At the beginning of the process, the SFT should develop a strategic document containing the following.

- A list of impacts and why they were chosen
- A brief illustration of the rolling strategic process
- A few more specific goals that have been broken out from the impacts as represented by goal statements (see Preparation for Change, page 99)

- An identification of which goals the team will address first
- Inputs and outputs for the goals for the coming year as the school enters the generation phase

This work initiates the rolling strategy process and starts the engine that will drive the work. It is not something that recurs in the same way year after year. After the SFT begins the process with this work, initiatives will emanate from the phases of the rolling process itself. Also, once the rolling strategy is in motion, the SFT begins to serve more as an oversight group, supporting and coordinating the actions across different initiatives, looking after consolidated resource needs, and helping assess the level to which initiatives have proven to be successful in achieving impacts.

Recall from figure 2.3 (page 27) that, while impacts are long-term in nature, outputs and inputs should change and progress across shorter time horizons. The following sections detail how the rolling strategic process may occur over the course of several years, as well as road-mapping tools that can help educators visualize and track plans and progress over time.

Year 1

The SFT has chosen one or two goals (let's call these *goal A* and *goal B*) to start with and has prepared them to enter the generation phase. In general, it is inadvisable to try to implement all your goals or impacts at once. However, through generation, design teams might develop solutions that can address more than one impact. In the first year, the generation phase will result in a program or strategy to address the goal and an action plan to move each goal into the execution phase in year 2.

The SFT decides that goal A is broad and complex and will need two years in execution. On the other hand, goal B is relatively self-contained and will need only one year in execution before moving to reflection. Also in year 1, the SFT identifies goal C and creates inputs and outputs to take goal C into the generation phase next year.

Year 2

Goal A and goal B should now have moved into the execution phase. The action planning from year 1 defines the work to undertake. At the same time, goal C moves into the generation phase. The SFT might decide on a fourth goal, or let the existing goals work through the phases. Perhaps halfway through the year, the SFT decides that goal C needs another year in generation. This is perfectly valid. The point is that you control the process and can be flexible within it.

SFT planning for year 3 will include deciding to keep goal A in execution for another year and refining its inputs and outputs for further implementation work. The SFT will also track inputs and outputs for goal B as it moves into reflection.

Year 3

During year 3:

- Goal A is completing the execution phase
- Goal B is in the reflection phase
- Goal C is completing the generation phase

SFT planning for year 4 and beyond includes moving goal A into reflection, wrapping up the efforts toward goal B and acting on recommendations from the reflection phase, planning for goal C to enter execution, and, perhaps, identifying and preparing for goal D based on what the SFT has learned and where the organization needs to go.

This actionable framework becomes an ongoing part of how the organization operates. It is important to reiterate that not all strategies should or would be in the same phase at the same time. This would create an unsustainable level of busyness, poorly implemented innovations, and a reduced ability to move forward based on new knowledge. The speed with which you launch new goals into the generation phase is completely within your control and should be sensitive to where you are, how far you've come, what you've learned, and the capacities of all concerned.

Road-Mapping

School environments and transformational goals are both extremely complex. One way schools can help make things more linear is through simple road-mapping. A road map is a simple visual showing actions across a timeline. It has proven helpful in my work by organizing the major actions and deliverables within a rolling strategic process for schools and districts. You can choose to organize your road map in different ways, two of which are shown in figures 6.3 and 6.4 (page 112).

Figure 6.3 simply maps work according to the goals in motion and what phase of the rolling strategic process they may be in for a given year. The small circles within the bars refer to the action plan created for that goal and year, where the number indicates a specific output and the letter indicates a specific input that is part of achieving the output. The map also indicates check-in or review points and points at which a goal-related decision needs to be made or approved.

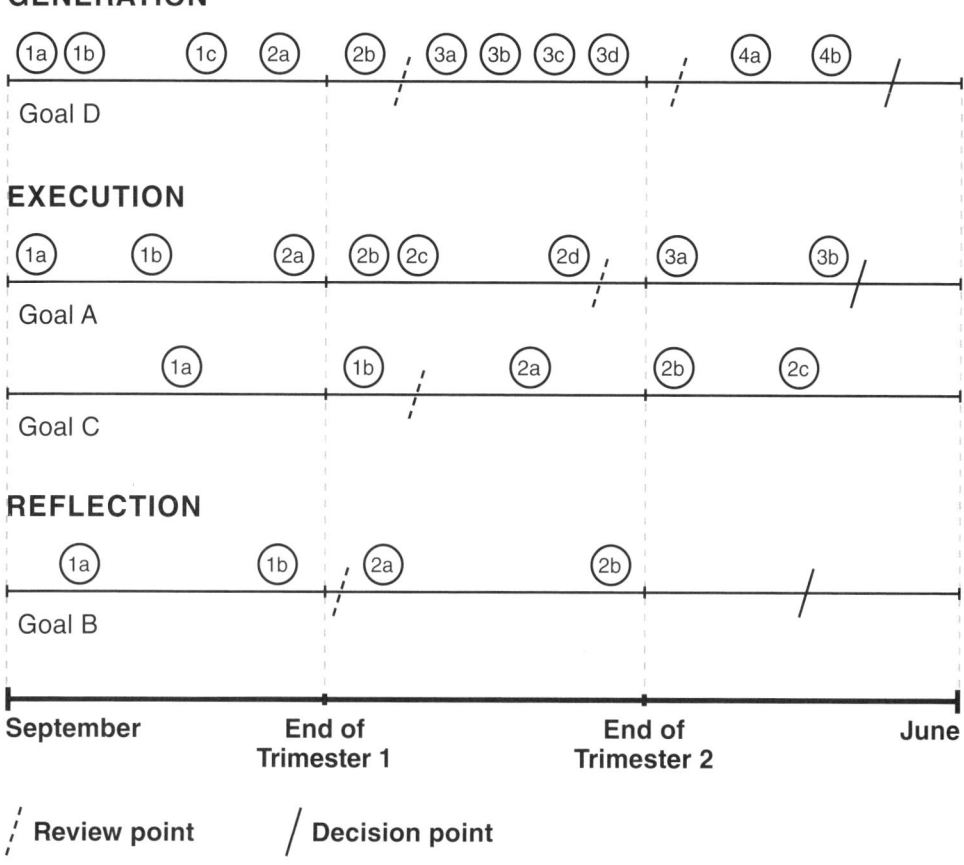

FIGURE 6.3: Road-mapping by goal and rolling strategic process phase.

The example in figure 6.4 (page 112) maps the work of various groups across the school year and includes a bar for a communication plan. The communication plan will include outputs and inputs as related to strategic communication with the entire community. You can organize your road maps in numerous ways, including with work streams (professional learning, teacher action, design, prototyping, implementation, and so on) and by departments or areas (curriculum office, professional development, leadership, elementary school, and so on). All of these will refer back to the original action-planning documents for the details.

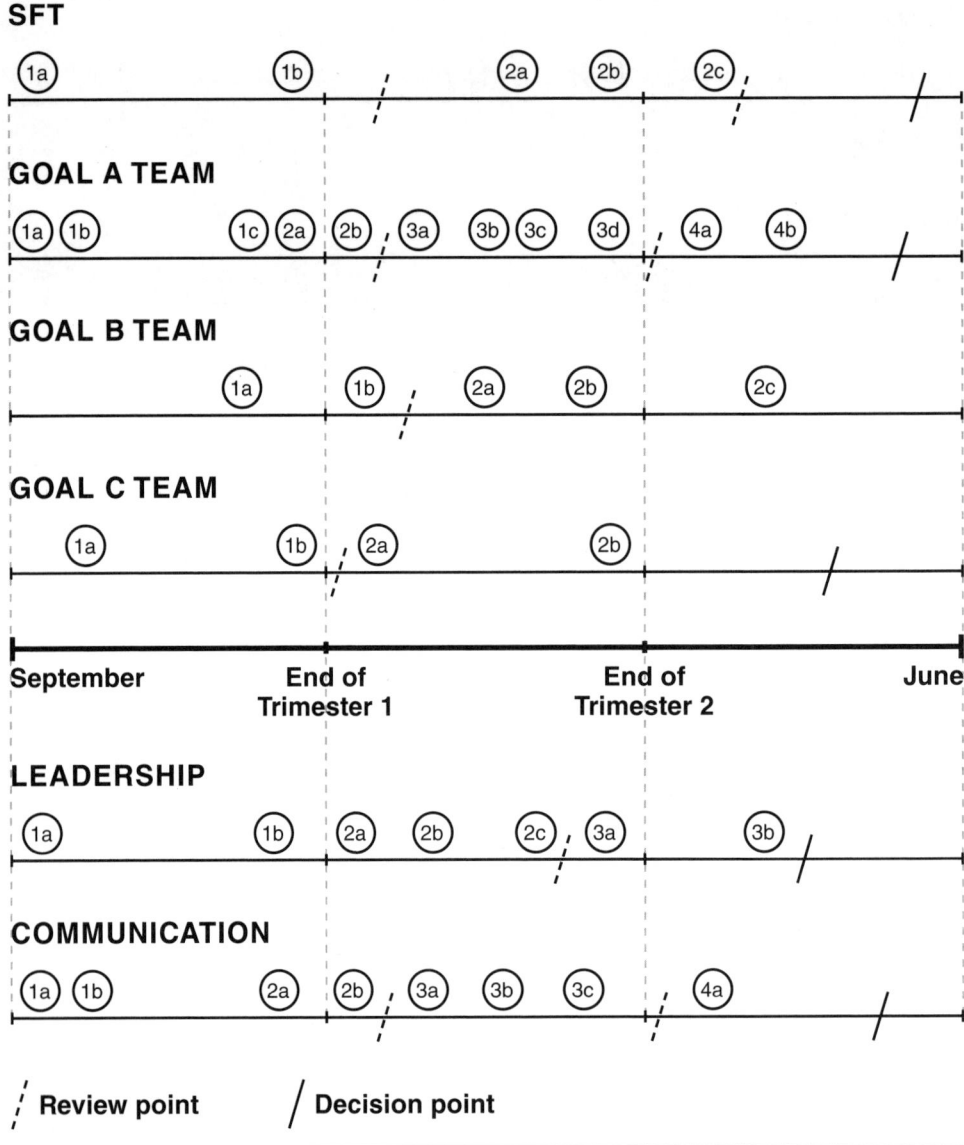

FIGURE 6.4: Road-mapping by working group.

In addition to illustrating the work on a timeline, developing simple road maps like this is beneficial because it gives you an easy way to make progress visible and to acknowledge the work that is being done. You could post this road map in the staff room or conference rooms, and each time an input is achieved, you could check it off. The road map could be colored in as various inputs and outputs are achieved to illustrate progress. Regardless of the precise method they use, organizations should find some way to organize the work, track progress, and celebrate accomplishments.

Two Tracks of Accountability

This book proposes that it is not enough to simply use the completion of inputs and outputs as evidence of our success at achieving our mission. Impacts provide the bridge between our mission and our actions. Ultimately, we do this work for our students' benefit—to help them become thriving, thoughtful, and contributing members of the world. When we see that they are becoming better equipped to do this and have had powerful learning experiences that have activated their unique attributes and dreams, that's our measure of success. If we have accomplished all of this, we also can look at our organization's progress, celebrate that progress, decide on next steps, and keep ourselves accountable to what's important. To do so, we should consider two tracks of accountability, represented by two questions: (1) Did we do what we said we were going to do? and (2) Are we progressing toward achieving our mission through our impacts? Both of these are easy to track when we have the systems and structures discussed in this book in place.

We must stop:

- Relying on check boxes of action steps accomplished as evidence of success and transforming learning
- Assessing completion of the plan instead of progress toward achievement of the mission and vision
- Using standardized scores as our only learning data and evidence
- Having a small group decide whether success has been achieved or progress made

Did We Do What We Said We Were Going to Do?

The first track of accountability simply tracks the completion of identified inputs and outputs. In fact, most schools typically include this information in annual reports on their strategic plan; they include lists of what the organization has done, facts and figures, and some anecdotes that attempt to tie these data to learning. Even if we move beyond this completion and track impacts, it's still important that we track the actions we hope will lead to those transformational effects. We can and should still track and report completion of the tasks in our plans. It acknowledges the work completed and the work ahead. If you put your goals and plans in the I-O-I format, you can easily accomplish this.

For reporting to the board of education, schools can use a simple visual that communicates progress and lets stakeholders know that things are on track—common visuals include dashboards with dials, gas gauges, and stoplights. Three or four times a year, they can present the board or other stakeholder groups with a simple chart that communicates, for each impact goal, the inputs and outputs that have been completed, are in progress, or are planned. Figure 6.5 features an example visual. Obviously, we want the visual to show significantly more completion over time. It also helps schools to show the progress chart from the previous reporting period so that the audience can see change over time. Optional content includes which phase of the rolling strategic process each goal is currently in and a list of inputs and outputs for each goal. Most often, however, audiences prefer a snapshot that shows things are progressing as planned or, if not, why not.

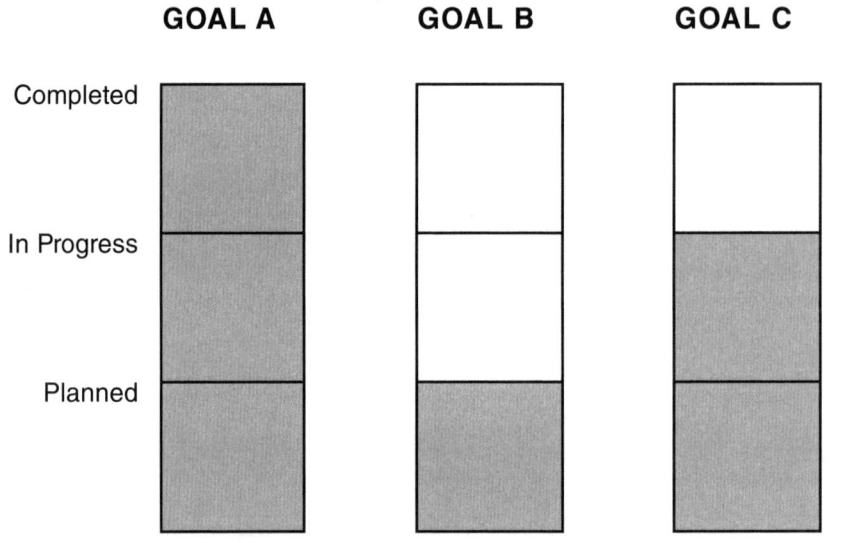

FIGURE 6.5: Input-output tracking visual.

Are We Progressing Toward Achieving Our Mission Through Our Impacts?

The importance of evidence and progress tracking has been an integral point of this book. In the context of implementing the rolling strategic process, two additional points are particularly salient.

1. For plans in the generation phase, you will not likely have a large pool of student learning evidence to draw on, as you haven't really begun to implement yet, and that's fine. You may have identified some desired

evidence for the prototyping process and refined these as suggestions within the action plan you submit, but you'll likely focus your measures of success on completion of inputs and outputs in this phase. Again, this is fine.

2. When it comes to assessing our actions' success in achieving our impacts, we need to take a step back. The strategic facilitation team needs to establish measures of success to use at an organizational level. Teachers greatly simplify this task if they have captured assessment feedback related to performance areas and impacts on an ongoing basis. Furthermore, the task is greatly aided by learning management systems, such as LearningBoard, that facilitate access to and analysis of relevant data. Schools should develop a succinct list of data that they will use on a regular basis to assess the organization's progress toward achieving impacts. This data menu may include the following.

- *Student assessment results*—We can draw these from regular assessment feedback and data over time.
- *Student self-assessment results*—If students are self-assessing their learning using the same impact scales as teachers, we can capture, organize, and analyze these data as well.
- *Student portfolios*—If students are regularly selecting, curating, interpreting, reflecting upon, and self-assessing evidence of learning (again, using the same scales as teachers), this provides us with a huge source of data.
- *Surveys*—Surveys can provide useful data, but we must ask the right questions and track changes over time. For example, if we ask fifth-grade students whether they feel they are good self-directed learners, we'll likely get a lot of yeses. This may not give us good evidence that our students are actually becoming more self-directed and good self-directed learners. Instead, we might ask students (at many age levels) to list their top five most powerful learning experiences from that school year. We would track the responses over time and hope to see the number of mentions of self-directed projects and experiences grow. This approach provides the evidence we want to point to the trend that we believe is positive, but it does so in a way that lends credibility to our conclusion.

The same can be said of climate surveys. Make sure that you clearly denote what would constitute evidence of success of a positive trend line, and carefully choose the questions you ask to elicit that feedback.

This data menu is rich and engaging. I encourage engaging the broader community in exploring this evidence in order to come to an agreement about progress made. Collecting evidence and tracking progress in this way can be inclusive and celebratory. When it is, it causes us to elevate our focus on student learning as evidence of success, engage people in looking at learning as the realization of our efforts, and energize ourselves to keep moving forward in a virtuous cycle. Schools have usually not provided this level of accountability, tracking, and reporting in the past. With I-O-I, we can separate our strategic actions from our strategic results in a much more authentic way.

It is important to note that we cannot measure organizational progress toward achieving impacts in a purely numerical way. There is no number on the scale that we can reach and say we are done. The key word here is *progress*. We can collect and analyze rich data, but realistically, we cannot put a finite number on the data, as we would, say, with a target of raising reading scores on a standardized test by 5 percent. It is more authentic to look at all the data and evidence collected and determine the level to which we have made progress. The scale for this progress might involve a simple set of increments ranging from *not at all* to *transformational* or whatever descriptors you choose. This scale is different from the ones used for assessment feedback; in this case, we are trying to communicate the level to which we believe that we've made progress.

As with input and output tracking, visuals that communicate this development convey important elements of progress and promote inquiry. A school team should create a visual at the end of each year and share it with the entire community as a simple assessment of the progress made in that year and over multiple years. Figure 6.6 displays a sequence of examples that communicate progress toward impacts over time. Each ray of the star represents an impact. The dots on each ray represent the verdict regarding the progress made toward the achievement of each impact—each dot is an increment on the progress scale. Over time, a star is superimposed for each year, so it's clear how long the goals have been in process.

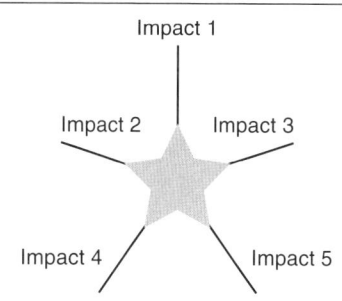	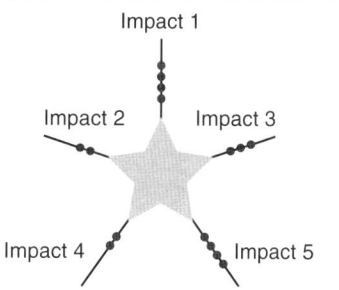
In year 1, we simply start where we are. Remember that baseline data are important to measure progress, but at this level, we don't need to say that our students started at 55 percent in global mindedness, 65 percent in critical thinking, and so on. Where we start is just where we start when we assess progress.	After the first year of serious evidence collection and interpretation, our impact data team or SFT should look at recent data and compare them with the baseline. Instead of trying to arrive at percentages of progress, the team should simply use increments (each dot represents an increment). This data team is tasked with analyzing the evidence and determining which level of our progress scale we've reached. We should trust the team with that work and its conclusions.
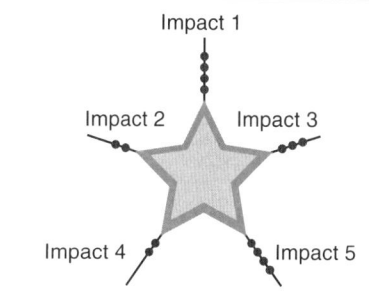	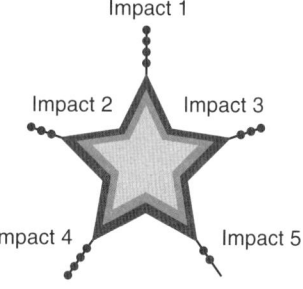
Once the team has rated our progress and plotted the increments on the rays of the star, we can add another star that illustrates another year of effort toward realizing each impact. In this way, we can easily see how long we've been working on the goals and how much progress we've made toward each one in the last year.	The following year, we can go through the process again. This time, we may see movement in different ways. Again, we need to interpret what this means. Perhaps impact 4 has really seen a boost as we've moved our plans for this into execution. Perhaps impact 2 seems to have benefited as well, as we found ways to address it alongside impact 4. Perhaps impact 5 has hit a wall and we need to address this. The important point is that the interpretation of progress should lead to insights that feed back into the strategic-thinking and action-planning process.

FIGURE 6.6: Communicating progress toward impacts over time.

Regardless of how you decide to track and report your success at addressing your mission, communicating progress is beneficial because it sustains your attention on strategically addressing impacts and communicates the positive result of everyone's efforts. This helps ensure that you do not forget impacts when a new fad comes in, but build them to last so they result in deep and meaningful transformations for your students. It's what makes all your efforts productive, rather than just busy.

Conclusion

This chapter described how we might make I-O-I part of organizational work on a regular basis. We explored the shift from the traditional strategic plan and toward an iterative form of strategic thinking and acting. Impacts drive this process, and I-O-I frames the necessary actions in clear, simple ways. Finally, we looked at evidence of success as an organization and how we might develop two tracks of accountability and reporting: (1) progress through our action plans and (2) progress toward the achievement of impacts. All of this represents years of concerted effort. It can be overwhelming if we do not think of the various stages of the rolling process and leverage I-O-I to support our thinking and planning. The processes and tools like road maps and visualizations help keep everything on track. When you think back on this and previous chapters, reflect on the process as one to carefully choreograph and facilitate. It may seem mechanical, but it has more nuance than first meets the eye, and the whole is greater than the sum of its parts.

Chapter 6 Resources

School and district teams can use the following questions and activities to put the concepts from this chapter into action. Teams should retain artifacts resulting from these exercises to inform later work.

Collaborative Inquiry

Consider the following questions, then discuss your answers as a team.

- Why is all of the work outlined so far in this book worth the effort? Which parts might be most important to you?
- How does our current method of communicating progress on our strategic plan work? How doesn't it work?
- How might we conduct something like this type of rolling strategic process?
- How do learning-focused goals change the game?
- What opportunities for community engagement and teacher leadership might we have available through this process?

Collaborative Activities

The following activities will help you and your team operationalize the ideas from this chapter. Each activity builds on the one before it, so we recommend completing them in the order shown. Be sure to review the instructions in advance and gather any needed materials, such as markers and chart paper.

Create a Visual

Using figure 6.2 (page 104) as an example, create a visual that demonstrates the relationship among the three phases of the rolling strategic process. Try to show the progression of goals through the phases over time. Use sample goals from the text or your own existing goals, and illustrate the transfer of energy and movement through the phases.

Reframe Your Goals

Most traditional goals have been written from an organizational point of view. They have focused not on learning but on the organization accomplishing something—an implementation, a facility, a teacher training, and so on. A shift in this focus can help you center on impacts as representative of your mission. Try the following in a small group.

1. Go to your strategic plan or whatever goal and planning documents you use.
2. Select a couple of goals stated therein. Attempt to reframe each goal as a learning-focused goal.
3. Consider what you notice about the nature of the goal, the action steps listed, and the evidence for reporting success.

Create an Evidence Menu

For each organizational impact, decide on the sources of data that would help the organization interpret its progress toward achieving its goals. Be specific about the data you plan to collect, but consider a wide range of sources.

Impact:		
Looking For What is our desired trend (what do we want the evidence to indicate over time)?	**Looking At** What evidence might we interpret?	**Evidence Source** Where and how might we collect this evidence?

Plan for Engagement

Page 121 shows a simple template to help align persons with the work to be undertaken in a given time period. As mentioned in chapter 6, strategic engagement of different community members and groups in different processes is an important change leadership strategy. Once you have outlined the outputs desired for each rolling phase, begin by asking the following questions.

- What skills and experience would help to create the best result?
- What is the ideal composition of the most effective and engaged group for this output?
- How do we offer engagement to important stakeholders?
- Who will be most impacted by the outputs of this process and should, therefore, be involved?

Rolling Strategic Process Phase	Planned Output	Who Should Engage in This Work?
Generation		
Execution		
Reflection		

EPILOGUE

By reaching the end of this book, you have demonstrated a commitment to exploring ways in which we, as educators, can reach higher. You may feel intimidated by the amount of work described, but know that it is useful work that can lead to meaningful and sustainable change for our learning communities. It is systematic work that focuses all activity on clear and important goals for learning. It is transformational work that will rein in the cycles of busyness that have plagued improvement efforts in education for so long.

I-O-I ensures that implementation efforts focus on the achievement of impacts. Beyond setting these lofty goals, I-O-I emphasizes that we must demonstrate, interpret, and assess our ability to help students achieve them. Laying the proper foundation for strategic thinking and actions keeps our efforts aligned with our goals. This, in turn, prevents the scattered implementation agendas that have created busyness with little satisfaction or lasting progress. Stick with it—this is long-term work, but it should not exhaust your organization or those who work within it.

Transformation is a multifaceted thing with many moving parts. It has no direct or singular pathway to success. We need to make purposeful change and develop a systematic approach to the work that will better serve our students. I-O-I is a set of interrelated structures, each initiated by the previous action and linked to the next one. It has a simple premise with broad and deep ramifications, if you commit to it and use it thoughtfully. While the premise may be simple, the processes of bringing it to fruition are varied and stretch over a long period of time. This book represents years of possible work for schools and districts. I-O-I is not a quick fix, but these ideas can lead to lasting transformation.

If the whole package of processes and activities described in this book doesn't fit you or your school, use it to catalyze your own thinking. An organization does not need to do all the activities or processes in this book—they can serve as suggestions, options, or inspirations. However, shortcutting too many processes might well water down the original framework too much and not lead to success. Educators must approach their work with care, intentionality, and fidelity.

It is my hope that the ideas, structures, and processes that this book has explored will help you find some avenues to move forward in your work. Our past approaches to strategic work and transformation have not proven very successful or lasting. Why not try some ways to do it differently, for our students and our schools?

APPENDIX

Sample Performance Areas for Impacts

Performance areas break broad impacts into identifiable elements. They help us clarify what we mean by a big term like *creative thinking* and develop a shared understanding of what impacts actually look like in our schools and classrooms. There is no definitive or complete set of performance areas for any given impact. It is important, however, that we demonstrate our future focus by selecting performance areas that operationalize impacts so students can put them into action. Table A.1 lists sample performance areas for a few common impacts. A good activity is to cut out a number of potential performance areas for your impacts and ask a small design group to sort and select the best ones for each impact. It usually leads to a very rich conversation, and it is an efficient way to come up with a short list.

Table A.1: Sample Performance Areas

Impact	Performance Areas
Creative Thinking	• Inquiry • Idea generation • Idea exploration • Idea application and execution • Design • Innovation • Exploration of needs and opportunities • Lateral thinking • Curiosity and imagination

Critical Thinking	• Inquiry • Conclusion generation • Meaning making • Analysis and interpretation • Innovation • Design • Need identification • Decision making • Systems thinking • Flexible thinking • Application of past knowledge to new situations • Conclusions testing
Collaboration	• Group membership skills • Interpersonal skills • Leadership • Followership • Contribution to group success • Productive group interactions • Effective group communications
Self-Directed Learning	• Reflection • Identity as a learner • Growth mindset • Goal setting • Self-advocacy • Resilience • Grit • Metacognition • Use of feedback
Global Mindedness	• Global awareness • Cultural literacy • Social intelligence • Citizenship • Considered decision making • Adaptability • Risk taking • Flexible thinking

Sample Performance Areas for Impacts

	• Systems thinking • Empathy • Initiative
Communication	• Expressive communication • Interpretive communication • Interpersonal communication • Aesthetics and presentation • Social interaction

REFERENCES AND RESOURCES

Barr, S. (n.d.). *Are you measuring something meaningful? How to avoid inert measures that anaesthetise your performance management.* Accessed at https://staceybarr.com/downloads/AreYouMeasuringSomethingMeaningful.pdf on March 18, 2019.

Barr, S. (2004, August 19). *Are you measuring something meaningful?* [Blog post]. Accessed at www.staceybarr.com/measure-up/are-you-measuring-something-meaningful on August 3, 2018.

Barr, S. (2010, May 17). *Why you can't measure your performance outcomes . . .* [Blog post]. Accessed at www.staceybarr.com/measure-up/are-you-measuring-something-meaningful on March 18, 2019.

Collette, M. (2015, March 5). A painful decade of school reform. *Slate.* Accessed at https://slate.com/human-interest/2015/03/reform-fatigue-how-constant-change-demoralizes-teachers.html on January 21, 2019.

Cuban, L. (2010, June 8). *The difference between "complicated" and "complex" matters* [Blog post]. Accessed at https://larrycuban.wordpress.com/2010/06/08/the-difference-between-complicated-and-complex-matters on May 23, 2018.

Curtis, G. (2018). *I-O-I: A simple formula for school transformation.* Accessed at https://commongroundcollaborative.org/i-o-i-a-simple-formula-for-school-transformation on April 1, 2019.

Enochson, H. (n.d.). *27 examples of key performance indicators.* Accessed at https://onstrategyhq.com/resources/27-examples-of-key-performance-indicators on August 3, 2018.

Exceptional Leaders Lab. (2017, April 5). *It's time to give Noel Burch some credit* [Blog post]. Accessed at http://exceptionalleaderslab.com/its-time-to-give-noel-burch-some-credit on June 26, 2018.

Fischer, B. (2016, November 26). The death of strategy. *Forbes.* Accessed at www.forbes.com/sites/billfischer/2016/11/26/the-death-of-strategy/#15e9d9567f99 on July 17, 2018.

Fullan, M. (2002). Moral purpose writ large. *School Administrator, 59*(8), 14–16.

Jacobs, H. H., & Alcock, M. H. (2017). *Bold moves for schools: How we create remarkable learning environments.* Alexandria, VA: Association for Supervision and Curriculum Development.

Loewus, L. (2017, December 19). Majority of teachers say reforms have been 'too much.' *Education Week.* Accessed at www.edweek.org/ew/articles/2017/12/19/majority-of-teachers-say-reforms-have-been.html on July 17, 2018.

Marr, B. (n.d.). *The 10 biggest mistakes companies make with KPIs.* Accessed at www.bernardmarr.com/default.asp?contentID=764 on July 23, 2018.

McTighe, J., & Curtis, G. (2016). *Leading modern learning: A blueprint for vision-driven schools.* Bloomington, IN: Solution Tree Press.

McTighe, J., & Curtis, G. (2019). *Leading modern learning: A blueprint for vision-driven schools* (2nd ed.). Bloomington, IN: Solution Tree Press.

Mendenhall, M. E., & Pryor, M. G. (n.d.). *Strategic planning failure.* Accessed at www.referenceforbusiness.com/management/Sc-Str/Strategic-Planning-Failure.html on July 23, 2018.

National Council for the Social Studies. (2013). *The College, Career, and Civic Life (C3) Framework for Social Studies State Standards: Guidance for enhancing the rigor of K–12 civics, economics, geography, and history.* Silver Spring, MD: Author.

National Governors Association Center for Best Practices & Council of Chief State School Officers. (2010a). *Common Core State Standards for English language arts and literacy in history/social studies, science, and technical subjects.* Washington, DC: Authors. Accessed at www.corestandards.org/assets/CCSSI_ELA%20Standards.pdf on March 26, 2019.

National Governors Association Center for Best Practices & Council of Chief State School Officers. (2010b). *Common Core State Standards for mathematics.* Washington, DC: Authors. Accessed at www.corestandards.org/assets/CCSSI_Math%20Standards.pdf on March 26, 2019.

New England Association of Schools and Colleges. (2018). *ACE accreditation protocol.* Accessed at https://cie.neasc.org/process/ace on March 12, 2019.

NGSS Lead States. (2013). *Next Generation Science Standards: For states, by states.* Washington, DC: National Academies Press.

Page, B. (2002). Swinging on the education pendulum. *Teachers.net Gazette, 3*(3). Accessed at www.teachers.net/gazette/MAR02/page.html on July 23, 2018.

Perkins, D. N. (2014). *Future wise: Educating our children for a changing world.* San Francisco: Jossey-Bass.

Perkins, D. N., & Chua, F. (2012). *Learning that matters: An expanding universe*. Cambridge, MA: Project Zero.

Price, R. (n.d.). *Why strategic plans don't work . . . and what to do about it*. Accessed at www.reliableplant.com/Read/15167/why-strategic-plans-dont-work-what-to-do-about-it on July 30, 2018.

Santoro, D. A. (2018). Is it burnout? Or demoralization? *Educational Leadership, 75*(9), 10–15. Accessed at www.educationalleadership-digital.com/educationalleadership/2018summer/MobilePagedArticle.action?articleId=1405586&app=false#articleId1405586 on August 2, 2018.

Schonert-Reichl, K. A., Lawlor, M. S., Oberle, E., & Thomson, K. (2009, April). *Identifying indicators and tools for measuring social and emotional healthy living: Children ages 5–12 years*. Vancouver, Canada: University of British Columbia. Accessed at www.jcsh-cces.ca/upload/SEL%20Report%20FINAL_May26.pdf on July 25, 2018.

Sinek, S. (2009). *Start with why: How great leaders inspire everyone to take action*. New York: Portfolio.

Tomlinson, C. A. (2018). One to grow on / Measuring doesn't come first. *Educational Leadership, 75*(5), 90–91.

Wiggins, G., & McTighe, J. (2005). *Understanding by Design* (2nd ed.). Alexandria, VA: Association for Supervision and Curriculum Development.

Wright, T. (2015, April 22). *7 top reasons why strategic plans fail* [Blog post]. Accessed at www.executestrategy.net/blog/7-top-reasons-why-strategic-plans-fail on July 17, 2018.

INDEX

A
academic feedback, 70–71
academic subjects, unpacking, 45–46
accountability, 113–118
    busyness from, 10
    distraction from mission and, 14
accreditation, 33–34
action planning, 92
    functions of, 102
agility, 26–27
Alcock, M., 40
alignment, 28
    of assessment, 85
    tool and strategy, 82–84
aspirations. *See* mission and mission statements; visions
assessment, 5–6
    accountability tracking, 114–116
    changing thinking about, 15–16, 61–63
    creating, 66
    data for, 115–118
    digital platforms, 76
    example of integrated, 73–76
    feedback in, 61–63
    for impacts, 26, 57–79
    integrating impacts with academic content, 65–69
    learning types articulation and, 57–60
    look-ats/look-fors in, 64–65
    making impacts assessable, 63–69
    performance indicators and, 48–50
    of progress, 116–118
    simplifying feedback for, 69–76
    standards-based, 70–71
    student self-, 115
    subject-area, 66
    systems design, 84–87

B
backward design, 2–3, 22
    tools and strategies with, 82–84
Ball, P., 30, 87, 108
Beijing City International School, 31–33
Bold Moves for Schools: How We Create Remarkable Learning Environments (Jacobs & Alcock), 40
Burch, N., 73
burnout, 10–11
busyness, 1–2
    change vs., 5
    cycles in, 10
    demoralization from, 10–11
    progress vs., 10

C
causality, 28
change, 3–4
    accountability tracking, 113–118
    busyness driven by, 1–2
    catalysts for, systems design and, 81–96

causality of, 28
    driving with impacts as goals, 69, 85
    establishing necessity of, 9–10
    facilitating, 97–121
    failure of most, 11–12
    fatigue from, 10
    how, 5, 39–56
    leadership, 106, 107
    planning for, 24–26
    preparation for, 99–102
    problems with traditional approach to, 9–20
    resistance to, 85
    road-mapping, 110–112
    strategic planning and, 14–17
    structuring based on I-O-I, 6
    what, 5, 21–38
    why, 5, 9–20
    why, what, and how of, 3–4
Change Leadership: A Practical Guide to Transforming Our Schools (Wagner & Kegan), 107
climate surveys, 116
coding, 62
cognitive skills, 58–59, 71
collaboration, 41
College, Career, and Civic Life (C3) Framework for Social Studies State Standards, 84
Collette, M., 10
communication, 106, 117–118
complexity theory, 28
content
    integrating impacts with, 65–69
    moving beyond, 40, 41
critical thinking, 41
    performance indicators for, 83–84
    tools and strategies for, 83–84
curriculum
    aligning with mission, 28
    embedding global issues into, 100
    impacts and, 23–24
    missions, visions, and, 12–13
    performance areas/indicators and, 50
    unpacking, 47

D

deep dives into implications, 85–87
demoralization, 10–11
digital platforms for assessment, 76, 115–116
dispositions, 23–24, 58–59
    feedback on, 73, 74
documentation of goals, 44

E

Eddington, M., 33
EdLeader21, 30–31
Education Week Research Center, 10
Elliott, L., 29, 97–98, 100
ends vs. means, 13–14
execution, 104, 106–107
    implementation timeline for, 109–110

F

feedback, 61–63
    academic, 70–71
    example of integrated, 73–76
    learning types and, 58
    performance area, 71–72
    qualitative, 61–62
    simplifying, 69–76
    specific, 63
Fifth Discipline, The: The Art and Practice of the Learning Organization (Senge), 107
"Four Stages of Learning Any New Skill" (Burch), 73
Fullan, M., 107
futility, sense of, 10
future, focus on the, 40–43

G

generation phase, 104, 105–106
    accountability tracking, 114–115

implementation timeline for, 110
global citizenship, 13
globalization, 43
global mindedness, 46, 47–48, 49, 60
goals. *See also* impacts
    aligning initiatives with, 2–3, 21
    aligning with mission, 28
    assessment and, 5–6
    clarifying, 43–45
    defining, 2–3
    failure of change efforts toward, 11–12
    future focus in, 40–43
    generation phase, 105
    identifying core transformational learning, 7
    identifying strategic facilitation team, 99–102
    impacts as, 69
    implementation timeline for, 108–112
    inputs and outputs for, 100–102
    mission, vision, and, 7
    moving beyond traditional, 40–41
    operationalizing, 7, 60
    operational vs. transformational strategic, 16
    overdocumenting vs. clarifying, 44
    road-mapping, 110–112
    statements of, 100
    unpacking, 45–46
grading scales, 70–71

H
habits of learning, 63
Heifetz, R., 107
how of change, 5, 39–56
    articulating learning types, 57–60
    assessing for impacts, 57–79
    clarify goals, 43–45
    designing systems around impacts, 81–96
    facilitating change, 97–121
    focus on the future, 40–43
    learning implications, 88–90
    making impacts assessable, 63–69
    operationalize impacts, 45–50
    shifting thinking about assessment, 61–63
    simplifying feedback practices, 69–76

I
IDEATE program, 31–33
Identifying Indicators and Tools for Measuring Social and Emotional Healthy Living (Schonert-Reichl, Lawlor, Oberle, & Thomson), 49
Immunity to Change: How to Overcome It and Unlock the Potential in Yourself and Your Organization (Kegan & Lahey), 107
impacts, 6, 11, 39–56
    accountability tracking, 113–118
    assessing for, 26, 47, 57–79, 61–63
    defined, 3, 22–23, 46
    descriptors of, 23
    designing systems around impacts, 81–96
    embedding, change driven by, 85
    examples of, 23
    goal statements on, 100
    implementation timeline for, 108–112
    inputs-outputs planning for, 100–102
    integrating with academic content, 65–69
    learning types and, 57–60
    making assessable, 63–69
    operationalizing, 45–50, 64
    performance areas and, 46, 47–48
    performance indicators and, 46, 48–50
    rubrics for, 70
    in subject-are assessments, 66

tools and strategies for, 82–84
unpacking and articulating, 45–47
implementation, 123–124
    accountability, 113–118
    assessment and, 15–16
    busyness driven by, 1–2
    driving with I-O-I, 26–34
    I-O-I framework for, 22
    perceived as goal, 11, 12, 15
    reflection on, 107–108
    road-mapping, 110–112
    in rolling strategic planning, 106–107
    strategic planning flaws in, 106
    timeline for, 108–112
Input-Output-Impact (I-O-I) framework, 2–3, 6, 123–124
    defining elements of, 21–24
    driving action with, 26–34
    facilitating change with, 97–121
    implications of for learning, 88–90
    implications of for systems, 84–88
    strategic facilitation teams and, 98–100
    student-centered approach in, 40
    supporting planning with, 24–26
    visual model of learning systems in, 90–92
inputs
    accountability tracking, 113–114
    defined, 3, 24
    in implementation timelines, 108–112
    measuring, 26
    planning for goals, 100–102
    road-mapping, 111–112
    in traditional strategic planning, 97–98
International School of Kenya (ISK), 90
I-O-I. *See* Input-Output-Impact (I-O-I) framework

J
Jacobs, H., 40

K
Kegan, R., 107
key performance indicators (KPIs), 26
knowledge base, 41, 42–43

L
Lahey, L., 107
Lawlor, M. S., 49
leadership, 106–107
Leadership on the Line: Staying Alive Through the Dangers of Change (Heifetz & Linsky), 107
Leading Modern Learning: A Blueprint for Vision-Driven Schools (McTighe & Curtis), 2, 41
learning approaches, 88–90
LearningBoard, 76, 115–116
learning environments, 89
    choosing pathways for, 89–90
    visual model of, 90–92
learning management platforms, 76, 115–116
learning types, 57–60
Linsky, M., 107
look-ats, 64–65
look-fors, 64–65

M
Marr, B., 16
McTighe, J., 2, 42–43
means vs. ends, 13–14
Mendenhall, M., 26–27
metrics
    for impacts, 61–63
    for inputs, 26
    for outputs, 26
mission and mission statements, 3, 7
    accountability tracking, 114–118
    aligning goals with, 21, 28

impacts and, 23–24
    operationalization of, 13–14
    practice vs., 12–13
    problems with, 12–14
    weasel words in, 13
Mott, P., 34

N

New England Association of Schools and Colleges' Commission on International Education, 33–34
Next Generation Science Standards (NGSS), 84
Nuance: Why Some Leaders Succeed and Others Fail (Fullan), 107

O

Oberle, E., 49
operationalization
    of goals, 7, 60
    of impacts, 45–50
    of mission/vision, 13–14
    transformational strategic goals vs., 16
outputs
    accountability tracking, 113–114
    choosing pathways for, 89–90
    defined, 3, 24
    in implementation timelines, 108–112
    measuring, 26
    planning for goals, 100–102
    road-mapping, 111–112
    in traditional strategic planning, 97–98

P

Page, B., 10
pathways, choosing, 89–90
peer review, 30–31
performance areas, 46, 47–48
    in assessment, 64–65
    defined, 46
    feedback on, 71–72
    for learning goals, 60
    learning types and, 58
    look-ats/look-fors for, 64–65
    rubrics for, 70
    tools and strategies for, 82–84
performance indicators, 26–27, 48–50
    critical thinking, 83–84
    defined, 46
    feedback based on, 62
    for learning goals, 60
    tools and strategies for, 82–84
performance labels, 70–73
Perkins, D., 40
portfolios, 115
predictability, 97, 98
prediction, 26–27
Price, R., 14
proficiency-based scales, 71–73
programmatic change
    additive vs. integrative, 2
    aligning goals with, 2–3
    busyness driven by, 1–2
progress
    busyness vs., 10
    tracking, 116–118
prototyping, 105–106
Pryor, M., 26–27

Q

qualitative research methodology, 62

R

reflection, 104, 107–108
    implementation timeline for, 110
reporting, 114, 116
road-mapping, 110–112
rolling strategic process, 27–28, 103–112
    accountability tracking, 113–118
    execution phase, 104, 106–107
    foundation principles for, 103
    generation phase, 104, 105
    implementation timeline, 108–112

phases, 104
reflection phase, 104, 107–108
road-mapping, 110–112
rubrics, 70
proficiency-based scales, 71–73
standards-based scales, 70–71

S

Santoro, D., 10–11
Schonert-Reichl, K., 49
School District of Greenfield, Wisconsin, 29–30, 86–87, 97–98
Senge, P., 107
SFTs. *See* strategic facilitation teams (SFTs)
shared understanding, 88–89
shortcuts, 123–124
Sinek, S., 3–4
skills, 42–43
impacts, 23–24
specific feedback on, 63
standards-based grading scales, 70–71
Start With Why: How Great Leaders Inspire Everyone to Take Action (Sinek), 3–4
STEP21, 30–31
strategic facilitation teams (SFTs), 98–100
implementation timeline by, 108–109
measures of success established by, 115–116
strategic planning, 14–17, 92
failure of traditional, 26–27, 97–98
failure points of, 106
goals of traditional, 97–98
implementation timeline, 108–112
with I-O-I, 24–26
oversight and facilitation of, 98–99
rolling strategic process vs., 27–28, 103–112
strategic plans, 97–98
strategic thinking, 6
stress, 10–11

surveys, 115–116
systems design, 81–96
choosing pathways in, 89–90
defined, 84
implications for, 84–88
implications for learning, 88–90
visual model of learning environments, 90–92

T

technology, 43
Thomson, K., 49
Tomlinson, C., 57, 61
tracking, 113–118. *See also* assessment
transdisciplinary learning, 58–59
transformation, 123–124
assessment of, 15–16
framework for effective, 2–3
operational vs. transformational goals and, 16

U

understanding, shared, 88–89

V

value conflict, 10–11
values learning, 58–59
visions, 3, 7
impacts and, 23–24
problems with, 12–14

W

Wagner, T., 107
what of change, 5, 21–38
driving with I-O-I, 26–34
inputs, outputs, impacts, 21–24
supporting with I-O-I, 24–26
why of change, 3–4, 5, 9–20
implementation and, 11–12
missions, visions, and, 12–13
strategic plans and, 14–17
workforce of the future, 42
working groups, 111–112
Wright, T., 26–27

Leading Modern Learning, Second Edition
Jay McTighe and Greg Curtis
Redesign education for 21st century learners with the support of *Leading Modern Learning*, second edition. More than a simple refresh, the latest edition outlines a reworked blueprint for major education reform and incorporates new insights, experiences, and tools for implementing modern learning practices.
BKF850

Swimming in the Deep End
Jennifer Abrams
Acquire the knowledge and resources necessary to lead successful change initiatives in schools. In *Swimming in the Deep End*, author Jennifer Abrams dives deep into the four foundational skills required of effective leadership and provides ample guidance for cultivating each.
BKF830

Time for Change
Anthony Muhammad and Luis F. Cruz
Exceptional leaders have four distinctive skills: strong communication, the ability to build trust, the ability to increase the skills of those they lead, and a results orientation. *Time for Change* offers powerful guidance for those seeking to develop and strengthen these skills.
BKF683

Flip This School
John F. Eller and Sheila A. Eller
Designed for administrators and teacher leaders, *Flip This School* presents a framework to lead a successful, sustainable school turnaround. Readers will gain a variety of practical strategies for planning school improvement efforts and collaborating with the existing staff to initiate a schoolwide transformation.
BKF669

Visit SolutionTree.com or call 800.733.6786 to order.

Wait! Your professional development journey doesn't have to end with the last pages of this book.

We realize improving student learning doesn't happen overnight. And your school or district shouldn't be left to puzzle out all the details of this process alone.

No matter where you are on the journey, we're committed to helping you get to the next stage.

Take advantage of everything from **custom workshops** to **keynote presentations** and **interactive web and video conferencing**. We can even help you develop an action plan tailored to fit your specific needs.

Let's get the conversation started.

Call 888.763.9045 today.

SolutionTree.com